W9-CPA-312

Simply put, I could not have run this race without Rhonda's support. This was my first race longer than a 10K, my first time in Africa, and my first time traveling this far alone. I felt comforted and supported every step of the way thanks to my newfound friend. She ran the first leg of the race with me and made me feel like I could really do this. We laughed together alongside our dream team Special Ops and made some unforgettable moments and really funny photos. I'm truly inspired by Rhonda and how much she's accomplished in the office and on the road. She's touched everyone she's met and left such an impression. So much so that people she had met in Singita on a previous vacation came miles away to cheer her on (and me with her!) as we crossed the finish line together. She's a fierce athlete with a big, strong heart. I was sick the second day, so did not run with Rhonda but on the third and final day, she said with conviction, "I want to finish this race with you!" And we did! We ran up that hill and posed in our sports bras like the proud New Yorkers we were! We were truly on top of the world, and I haven't stopped smiling since.

MARIETTA ALESSI
Social Media Manager, *Shape & Fitness* Magazines

As human beings, we all have the potential to achieve our dreams. All we have to do is stop setting limits on our dreams and start actually doing what needs to be done. There's no substitute for knowing deep down that you can handle anything that shows up...anything. With insight and grace, Vetere's Grit & Grind shows you how. I'm going to go read it again.

PAUL BARRETT, PHD, CPA
Deputy Director, Center for Business and Human Rights at New York University

We all have the potential to reach great heights and realize our dreams. Success, however, takes grit, perseverance, and determination. Nobody understands this process better than Rhonda Vetere. This book shows you how to get your hands dirty and achieve goals you thought impossible. A must-read!

WHITNEY BOWE, MD
Celebrity Dermatologist, TV Personality & Author of Best-Selling Book
The Beauty of Dirty Skin

This book is magic for anyone looking to develop more confidence in themselves. Believing is the key, and no one believes in the power of grit and grind more than Rhonda Vetere. Rhonda is a constant inspiration in the boardroom. Let her inspire you in your room.

CHERYL CASONE
Anchor at Fox Business Network, Author of *The Comeback: How Today's Moms Reenter the Workplace Successfully*

Within one hour, anyone who meets Rhonda knows her authenticity, positivity, and ability to both solve problems and inspire others!

MIKE CHAMPION
Founder & CEO of Xcelocloud

Grit & Grind takes on the pervasive illusion that there is an easy path to achieve worthwhile goals. The truth is that the road to success is long, requiring stamina and determination. Over her career, Rhonda has found 10 principles that have been instrumental not only to her success, but also for the organizations she has led. These principles are simple yet illuminating, and provide a roadmap that anyone can use to reach their goals.

SASHA COHEN
Figure Skater, Olympic Silver Medalist, 3x World Championship Medalist, Grand Prix Final and US Champion

A beautifully simple way to confidently reach whatever goals you set for yourself—at work, at home, anywhere in your life. This book will show you how.

OWEN DAVIDSON
International Tennis Hall of Fame, 4x US Open and Wimbledon Champion, 2x Australian Open Champion, French Open Champion

We all want life to be perfect and easy. But the real world doesn't work that way. Rhonda's 10 principles have seen her through some of the world's biggest crises in the past 2 decades. Grit & Grind shares the principles that guide her global teams to success.

VERONICA DAY
Team USA Skeleton Athlete and International Medalist

Read this book. Really. Wherever you are, whatever goals you're trying to achieve—you need the lessons Vetere lays out so gracefully, like the technology icon she is. Life is messy, so get your hands dirty!

JAY FERRO
CIO, Global Executive

A beautiful yet simple way to build a solid foundation of confidence that helps individuals reach the goals they have set for themselves—whether it's at work, home, or anywhere else in their life. Rhonda has been inspirational and strives to create an impactful difference in their success.

JAGADESHWAR GATTU
Corporate Vice President, HCL Technologies

If there is one person I have worked with who knows how to dig deep and get what they want, it's Rhonda Vetere. Rhonda doesn't settle for the easy way out. She is one of the most people-oriented persons I have met in the world. She is determined and focused, and helps others get what they want. She has a massive amount of energy and passion with a huge heart. Rhonda's experience, insights, and teachings are world-class. It's very exciting to see Rhonda share the principles in this book to help you succeed. Thank you, Rhonda, for being the ultimate leader and making a difference!

DENIS GIANOUTSOS
CEO Leading Change Partners, Executive Coach, Facilitator and Speaker

I have read plenty of books promising big successes. They focus on superficial tips rather than helping you unleash your true potential. Rhonda Vetere's book is totally different from all the others because she uncovers the incredible strength of the human spirit. This book is not about showing you an easy way to avoid the hard work. It's about how you can build your success with passion and dedication and, against all odds, you can actually achieve. Rhonda herself is a perfect example of that. She is an authentic leader, with whom I had the privilege to work and learn so much from. I'm very grateful for having Rhonda in my life, and for receiving this miraculous gift of Grit & Grind.

RENATA KRUTILNIKOW
Senior Operations Manager at HCL Technologies

If ever there were a personification of the words grit and grind, it would be Rhonda! She is not just an inspirational business leader who has been a path breaker in so many ways, but is also a wonderful human being who goes out of her way to share her gifts with the rest of the world.

KALYAN KUMAR
CVP & Chief Technology Officer at HCL Technologies

Rhonda is one of the most ambitious, organized, happy, forward-thinking women of her time. Her drive is the element that true leaders possess and cultivate. I am very honored to have her in my life and very proud to call her a close friend. She probably ran a half marathon and answered a few hundred emails in the time it took me to write this.

ROB LABRITZ
PGA Professional and Director of Golf at Glen Arbor Golf Club

All human beings have the potential to reach great heights, if they just stop trying to avoid what actually needs to be done. There's no substitute for knowing deep down that you can handle anything if you just roll your sleeves up and get engaged. This is a must-read book for anyone wanting to and willing to take action and make a difference. Rhonda Vetere has done this her whole life, and she lays out how you can too!

BRENDAN LYNCH
President and CEO, Eastern Computing Exchange, Inc.

As Rhonda's best friend since we were three years old, I've had the pleasure of watching her grow into the passionate visionary and iconic business-woman she is today. She has never stopped working hard and looking out for others. Through the years, we have shared many adventures around the globe, and I am so proud of the woman she is today. As I have always said, nobody works harder or smarter!

MICHELLE MADISON
Best Friend, Supermodel, TV Personality, Nurse

Grit & Grind takes on one of the most damaging beliefs of the modern age—that everything is supposed to be perfect and easy. The truth is that success takes time and determination, and yes grit. Rhonda Vetere has played a part in solving many of the world's biggest messes over the last 20 years. She uses these 10 principles to guide her global teams to success, and you can too.

ELANA MEYER
Olympic Silver Medalist, Long-Distance Runner

Grit & Grind is a must-read! We all know by now that success takes time and determination. Rhonda Vetere is a true role model who has played a part in solving many of the world's biggest messes over the last 20 years. She uses these 10 principles to guide her global teams and her mentees (like myself) to success, and so can you.

IMAN OUBOU
CEO and Founder of SWAAY Media, Former Miss New York 2015

She's a badass...a Gucci Gangster, Prada Princess, Yves Saint Laurent Don, Black Ops Assassin. Kicking @$$ and taking names! Grit & Grind aptly describes Rhonda's tenacious style and her successful career. Intractable problems are always her priority. Where others play it safe from the side-lines, Rhonda digs in, gets dirty, and lives the mission with her team, driving collaborative environments through fierce loyalty, collective innovation, and shared sacrifice. Success is the only outcome.

JP ROSATO
CEO of Sitehands

Sometimes in life you need a push—a mentor and a leader to give you direction and self-determination to achieve success. In my case, I was an extreme introvert and was living an ordinary, directionless life. But one fine day, Rhonda came to lead our organization like a breath of fresh air. She came with institutional knowledge, super leadership qualities, great mentorship skills, and infectious energy and laughter. Everything changed after she joined us—our work style, the way we talked, our social engagement, and our thought processes. It all started by reflecting her 10 guiding principles.

These principles taught me to work as a team, to believe in myself, to work toward achieving the impossible, accountability, determination, and how to stay fit and healthy. (With Rhonda on the floor, one could expect 4 am meetings at the gym.) Rhonda has the purest heart and soul I have ever come across in my life. Whatever I am today professionally is because of her. As she says, "There's no fun in dreaming alone; dreaming together makes a difference."

KULBHUSHAN "KB" SHARMA
Executive Director, Global Security Architecture, Engineering & Operations at Estée Lauder Companies

Rhonda is an inspiration for women's empowerment. She is strong and humble, and this book mimics just that. Grit & Grind shows that you can achieve anything you set your mind to. With a little grit and a little grind, you can be your own boss. Rhonda has accomplished so much in her life, and now she is giving us the chance to get inside her thoughts. This book is a must-read. I know I have taken in her wisdom to help me succeed as a professional athlete.

ERIN STORIE
Professional Triathlete Olympian

There are people who talk and there are people who do. Rhonda is a do-er! When a challenge is presented in the business world or in her personal life, she rolls up her sleeves and just gets it done.

PETER TRIZZINO
Senior Vice President, Worldwide Global Accounts at Dell EMC

To anyone who's stuck, frustrated, facing challenges, or wondering why life isn't insta-easy, take heart. It's time to roll up your sleeves and get your hands dirty. Yes, even more than they already are. I've personally seen how these 10 principles have guided Rhonda's global teams to success. Take them to heart, and you'll have a solid foundation to help you handle anything life can throw your way.

RAY WANG
Principal Analyst & Founder, Constellation Research, Inc.

I highly recommend this book! If you are looking for guidelines, inspirations, or blueprints for a successful life, this is it. Rhonda herself is a perfect example of these 10 life principles. She is not afraid to roll up her sleeves to get her hands dirty when faced with life's challenges. She has shown grit and perseverance over and over again in her over 20 years of leadership. Rhonda is an inspiration for men and women who want to live an extraordinary life. And this book reflects all her beliefs and what it takes! Love it!

VERA VIVIONA WANG
Global Fashion Icon, Founder of Miss Fashion Week

In my modeling and television career, I have encountered some of the world's most creative and cutting-edge minds. Rhonda outshines them all. Her commonsense approach to problem solving and innovation is second to none. She truly inspires me and has the biggest heart.

ROSHUMBA WILLIAMS
Supermodel, TV Personality

GRIT & GRIND

10 PRINCIPLES FOR LIVING AN EXTRAORDINARY LIFE

Rhonda Vetere

Print ISBN: 978-1-944602-21-5
Ebook ISBN: 978-1-944602-27-7

Thanet House Publishing
848 N. Rainbow Blvd. #750
Las Vegas, NV 89107

Cover Design and Interior Layout by Danielle Foster
Edited by Julie Willson

FOR DISCOUNTED BULK SALES, CONTACT Sales@ThanetHouseBooks.com

Publisher's Cataloging-In-Publication Data
(Prepared by The Donohue Group, Inc.)

Names: Vetere, Rhonda, author.
Title: Grit & grind: 10 principles for living an extraordinary life/Rhonda Vetere.
Other Titles: Grit and grind
Description: Las Vegas, NV : Thanet House Publishing, [2019]
Identifiers: ISBN 9781944602215 (print) | ISBN 9781944602277 (ebook)
Subjects: LCSH: Vetere, Rhonda--Career in technology. | Self-confidence. |
Persistence | Success--Psychological aspects. | Quality of life. |
High technology industries--Management.
Classification: LCC BF575.S39 V48 2019 (print) | LCC BF575.S39 (ebook) |
DDC 158.1--dc23

THANET HOUSE
PUBLISHING

*Dedicated to anyone facing a challenge
and trying to find their way through it.*

*May you discover the incredible strength your spirit holds
and use it to overcome whatever stands in your way.*

The credit belongs to the man who is actually in the arena...
who at the best knows in the end the triumph of high achievement,
and who at the worst, if he fails, at least fails while daring greatly,
so that his place shall never be with those cold and timid souls who
neither know victory nor defeat.

— THEODORE ROOSEVELT

CONTENTS

INTRODUCTION

All I wanted to do was hide under the blankets and pretend it wasn't morning yet. At 10 years old, I was already hearing "Olympic team hopeful" tossed around by my swim coaches and trainers. Day after day, my alarm clock sounded in the wee hours of the morning to wake me up for swim practice. I loved swimming, but I didn't love mornings. What kid does? Dragging myself out of bed almost every day to hit the pool was exhausting. Did I want to be an Olympian, or did I want sleep? Swimming was consuming my life, and as a kid, I wasn't ready for the kind of commitment and sacrifice it would take to become an Olympic swimmer.

Eventually, I quit swimming. Although I spent many years afterward as a lifeguard, I didn't enter the pool again as a swimmer for another 30 years. Life went on. I got busy with other things—school then college then my career. I found myself working insane hours in stressful situations, and I didn't allow myself the mental space to process work and life. I wasn't sure how to build that space into my life. I just knew I needed it.

I'd always been an athlete, so I turned to running as a way to clear my head. I call it my active meditation time. Through training for races and marathons, I became interested in triathlons, and that's when I found myself poised on the edge of the pool, ready to dive back in. As I fell into a cadence with the calm quiet of the water and nothing but my breathing in my ears, I knew I'd stayed away from swimming for too long. I was home again.

Now on the weekends, my alarm goes off at 4:30 am. No, that's not a typo. I plan my race schedule a year in advance, and it seems like my next race is always just around the corner. I have three or four hours of training ahead of me this morning, so I pat my cat on the head, throw back the covers, and roll out of bed. As tempting as it is to just sleep a little bit longer, I won't. Training is my safe space. It's what keeps me sane.

I guess you could say I'm a corporate athlete too. As a chief technology and chief information officer for major worldwide corporations, my team and I are the ones they call in when everyone else is walking out. I deal in stress with a capital S on a daily basis. We keep things together when no one else can. My executive style and physical training style mirror each other, and I think that's a huge part of how I've been able to deal with some of the challenges my team and I have faced.

I've been boots-on-the-ground during some of our century's biggest threats, like the events of 9/11, nuke testing in the demilitarized zone in Korea, and the demonetization of currency in India. I've crawled through tunnels with fiber-optic cables in my hands, performed tense negotiations with all-male executive boards for international companies, and narrowly escaped being kidnapped in India. I've completed five Ironman 70.3 Triathlons on extreme courses in extreme conditions, 60+ half marathons, marathons, and triathlons. I kept people from jumping out of windows during the Lehman Brothers financial collapse and ran through the Serengeti with a contingent of armed guards.

People often ask me how I got to where I am today and how I handle the stressful situations I deal with on a daily basis. How did I go from being a preteen who prioritized sleep over an Olympic career to being someone who's made a career out of jumping into corporate messes with both feet and getting up at 4:30 am on the weekends to train for 70.3-mile races?

I did it by making grit and grind the process for my life.

It's not WHAT challenges you face in life but HOW you face them that matters. Let's be real—there's no such thing as a struggle-free, perfect life. It's not IF you'll face challenges, it's WHEN. No one can just sail through life and avoid the messes. And whether each challenge is big or small, life-altering or merely an inconvenience, you don't get to choose your struggles. That doesn't mean you have NO choice though. In fact, it's when the challenges come and the going gets rough that we get to make some of the most important choices of all. We get to choose how we handle them.

There are basically only three ways people deal with challenges—avoid them, go around them, or plow straight through. Some people try to avoid challenges at all costs.They prefer the easy road, and they'd rather refuse to grow and develop than face anything that might be painful or make them uncomfortable. Others seek the shortest path around their challenges by passing the buck, sweeping things under the rug and refusing to deal with them, or bailing on a situation when the going gets tough. Those so-called shortcuts rarely turn out well in the long run.

When it comes to real life, avoidance and shortcuts will get you nowhere but stuck. Whether you're seeking success at work, dealing with a health crisis or injury, or just trying to get "unstuck" in some area of your life, the quickest way to get to the other side is to dive into the mess and learn your way through it.

And you WILL get through it.

Humans have an innate desire to grow and expand. That means we have desires and goals. And we have to work our way through the challenges to make those goals happen. There's no way around it. You can take the slow way and avoid the inevitable. Or you can dive in and get through it as quickly as possible. Not just once. Every time.

You're stronger than you know. You're more capable than you give yourself credit for. No matter what challenges you face, no matter how messy things get, you CAN work your way through them, and things WILL be better on the other side. When you're not afraid of getting your hands dirty, and when you embrace the idea that some challenges might even be fun, nothing can stop you from achieving the life you desire.

It doesn't matter where you start. And it doesn't matter what your goals are.

You might want to finish school...or to just finish the day without fighting with your spouse.

You might want to start a business...or to start your first job.

You might want to escape poverty...or to liberate yourself from an abusive relationship.

The 10 principles in this book will help you develop the skills to handle whatever life throws your way while building bone-deep confidence in your own abilities. And when you gain that confidence, you'll not only survive through the grit and grind, you'll lead others through too.

You'll learn you can do more than you ever dreamed.

You'll find you can overcome the seemingly impossible.

And you'll meet amazing new friends who become like family along the way.

You can't tell me that's not worth it.

If you go all-in, you'll experience tremendous growth and change in your leadership style, even if the only person you're leading is yourself.

Welcome to being truly alive.

TWO SIDES OF THE COIN

I've never really done things the easy way. It's something my mother trained into me back when I was just a kid. If I wanted something, I had to work for it—nothing was handed to me. I worked all through high school and college, paying my own way through. If I thought things were going to get easier when I graduated and started my career, I was wrong. My professional mentor immediately started placing me in leadership roles in industries where women were few and far between. At first, I thought he was being unreasonable, but eventually I realized there was a very purposeful plan behind his guidance.

My mentor saw potential in me that I didn't see in myself. That's when I began to realize that one of the biggest obstacles I was going to have to work to overcome in navigating adversity and challenges was actually...
well...me.

Sensible Rhonda vs. Full-Contact Rhonda

Once you decide to dive in, don't be surprised if you start feeling like you're in the middle of a battle—with yourself. An internal back and forth takes place between the sensible side of you and the risk-taker. Challenges have a way of intensifying both sides, and you may vacillate between "Yikes! Can I really do this?" and "Yes, I'm unstoppable! I can do anything!!" This is completely normal, and I go through it too. In fact, let me introduce you to two important women in my life: Sensible Rhonda and Full-Contact Rhonda.

Sensible Rhonda is a great gal. She's got a really level head about her, and she always knows to weigh in on the side of caution. In fact, now that I think about it, she sounds an awful lot like my mother. Sensible Rhonda is a voice of reason, but she doesn't always enjoy taking risks or jumping into the messes of life. Sensible Rhonda says, "I should NOT dive off that cliff. That could be dangerous. I could get into an accident and severely injure myself, and I'm too busy to deal with an injury. I'd better just stay home."

It's not a far-fetched concept. I HAVE been injured during races before. I was once injured after being hit by another racer's bike, getting my leg caught in the bike chain.

On the other hand, Full-Contact Rhonda is a powerhouse. She's always up for a challenge, and no one could accuse her of being dull. Full-Contact Rhonda really thrives in stressful situations. She's resilient, and she's great in a crisis, because she's quick to take action. But she can be kind of unpredictable, and it's hard for her to rein it in when she needs to.

Full-Contact Rhonda says, "Oh come on. I should TOTALLY go cliff diving. I'll just go beast mode and knock it out of the park. You only live once. What's the worst that could happen?" There have been times when that kind of attitude has gotten me through some major challenges that could have knocked me down. Instead Full-Contact Rhonda rose up and I pushed through.

I need both Sensible Rhonda and Full-Contact Rhonda in my life. In fact, I can't live without them. They create a balance in a way that going all-in on one or the other could never do. If I let Sensible Rhonda completely take over, I'd be living my life on the sidelines, too hesitant to jump into the race and take the risks that need to be taken. If Full-Contact Rhonda took over, I'd be going kamikaze on everything and burning bridges, and I wouldn't be the steady, trustworthy kind of leader people need. Together, my two Rhondas give off a balance of creative caution, prepared power, and strategic action that I can harness to get the best results in any situation.

Although I was terrified when my mentor put me in positions I didn't feel ready for, I went for it anyway. I'm so glad I did. Jumping into the messes time and time again gave me experience I'd never have gotten any other way. During the course of my career, I've seen just about everything there is to see. I've seen major corporations and world financial frameworks rise and fall. I've seen leaders—both good and bad—come and go. And challenges as far as the eye could see. But with each challenge overcome, both my sensible and full-contact sides learned and grew in confidence.

Over time, I began to notice there was a pattern and a cadence to how successful people navigated adversity and rose above the struggles they faced. Certain principles appeared again and again as hallmarks of success, and as I came across them, I picked them up and implemented them as practices in my life. I also began sharing them with my teams. Those hallmarks are the 10 principles this book is based on, and I share them with my teams all over the world.

The legacy of these principles lives on, all over the world. To this day, the list hangs in offices in China, India, London, Poland, and Hong Kong. In fact, someone from Poland recently sent me a photo of these 10 principles painted on the wall of their office.

The 10 principles of grit-and-grind living can be applied to any area of life. You don't have to be a corporate executive like me to use them. You can put them into practice as a college student gearing up to enter the workforce, a parent looking for a way to manage your household effectively while building meaningful relationships with your kids, or as a committee member on a local nonprofit board.

Discipline: Your Key to Freedom

It takes discipline and consistency to start seeing results with these 10 principles. It's not glamorous, but it's true. It's kind of like how I train for races. People assume my goal is to win one someday or have the best time. The truth is, I run races because I find joy in doing them. When I first started training, it wasn't easy...or fun. But as my body got stronger and I grew in endurance, running became my active meditation and thinking time. Training is a discipline, and now that I'm older, I understand that discipline is a gift that spills over into every area of my life. Triathlons are an outlet for me to practice discipline, and along the way they've become some of the most enjoyable experiences of my life. Every time I lace up my running shoes, hop on my bike, or dive in the pool, I'm building strength that carries over into every aspect of my life, and it benefits me at home, at work, and anywhere in the world I travel.

Discipline isn't always used in a healthy, positive way though, is it? Sometimes we keep doing things because they make us feel noble or superior somehow or because we want to please or impress someone else. Like playing the piano every day because your mom always wanted you to be a musician. Or spending 12 years becoming a doctor because that's what your dad and grandfather did (even though you wanted to be a novelist). Practicing discipline like this doesn't free us, it creates our own prison. When you lock yourself into something out of habit or ease, or as a way to gain a measure of love and approval from people that you depend on for your self-worth, you just keep doing it. Do you hear the lock clicking in the prison cell of your own making?

It takes guts to embark on the journey to what you really want, and you have to guard against becoming your own worst enemy. When you think about that one thing you've always wanted to do, your sensible side is quick to rear her head.

It's just not practical. I'm too old. It's dangerous. Maybe someday, but not today.

We're so good at using discipline as an excuse to keep us stuck in something that was never our purpose to begin with. Meanwhile, your full-contact side is protesting mightily.

Now is my chance. I must seize the day. I may never get another opportunity to do what I was meant to do. I've got to take the risk—my time is now!

Who are you going to listen to? How will you find the right balance?

Discipline can be the key to freedom or the key that locks you in your prison forever. It just depends on your perspective and who you allow to hold the key. This book can help.

Consistently putting the 10 principles in this book into action builds character, giving you a foundation for whatever you'll face next. No matter who you are or what you do, the more you practice grit and grind, the more you can be present in the moment, meditate on it, and learn from the process. The action of living these practices every day positively impacts your life. Discipline gives us a way to track our progress, celebrate our successes, and grow. What freedom we can experience in that!

The best way to leave a mark in this world is to get your hands dirty.

1

BE PREPARED
How Not to Get Kidnapped in India

You never really appreciate how vital it is to be prepared until you're not. There's only so much a person can handle by winging it. And in my world, not being prepared can have a steep, steep price. A price I may not be prepared to pay.

I was in my twenties when I went to India for the first time. It was there I had a dream-come-true experience. I was a global business woman, living and working in a foreign land. It was heaven. But one moment of not being prepared almost put me in my own personal hell.

If you've ever been to Mumbai, you know that it's a melting pot of sound and color and activity. Being out in the streets energized me, but I was there for work. So I spent most of my time in corporate meetings. When I finally did have an afternoon free, I knew exactly how I wanted to spend it.

Shoe shopping.

The shopping in Mumbai was unlike anything I'd ever seen. A few days earlier on the way to a meeting, I'd passed by a shop and my mouth dropped open. It looked amazing, and I knew that was the first place I'd head as soon as I had a chance.

You have to understand something about me and shoes. I LOVE shoes. Some people love cars. Some people love jewelry. For me, it's shoes and purses. I have a whole room in my house devoted to them. No way I was leaving India without doing some serious shoe shopping.

Around 2:00 pm that day, I threw on some sweats and grabbed my big sunglasses. I didn't bother applying makeup or doing my hair. The only people I knew who would see me were my driver and two bodyguards supplied by the company I worked for, and they didn't care what I looked like.

It every bit as magical as I'd hoped it would be. The walls were lined with shoes in every size, style, and color. There was a gentleman upstairs literally handing down shoes in my size through the ceiling as fast as he could. All I could think was, *This is really happening! Heaven is raining shoes from the sky!*

Since I go all-in with everything I do in my life, shopping is no exception. When I walked out of that store, my arms were full, loaded down with all the shoes I'd bought. As I stepped out of the shop, I was hit with everything that is Mumbai. Traffic was insane. It was dirty and loud and chaotic, and these guys right outside the door were yelling, "Hollywood! Hollywood!"

My driver had parked the car in an alley nearby. All I had to do was get to it, but somehow I got turned around. Which alley was he in? Was it to my left or to my right? Everything looked different, and I couldn't think with all the men shouting, "Hollywood! Hollywood!" What did that even mean? Who the heck were they yelling at?

Suddenly, a man stepped out and grabbed me, and I realized they had been yelling at me.

I wish I could say I went into some amazing martial arts scene like in the movies, but the truth is I just froze. I couldn't swing my arms full of bags. Instead of throwing them down and fighting for my life, all I could think to do was dig my heels into the ground and pull against them, screaming, "STOP! NO! I'm not...I'm not going with you!"

"Hollywood! Hollywood! Hollywood!"

I was surrounded by several men, who all grabbed my arms and pushed me down the alley.

"HOLLYWOOD! HOLLYWOOD! HOLLYWOOD!"

A car appeared suddenly and I realized with horror that they were going to shove me into it.

I twisted and tugged harder, trying to escape their grasp. Panic crawled up my chest and into my brain. This could not be happening. "NO! Let me go! STOP IT!"

Suddenly, I heard a different voice screaming from the other end of the alley. To this day, I can still hear the sound of my driver bellowing, "You're not taking her! You're not taking her!"

It was the most beautiful thing I'd ever heard. One of my bodyguards barreled through the crowd and punched the guy on my left, the other guard right on his heels. The kidnapper let go of me, and I dropped all the shoes. My driver clutched the other guy by the collar and threw him to the ground. My bodyguards whisked me to our car, and before I could even process what was going on, I was headed toward my hotel and safety.

It all happened so fast. Afterward all I could think was, *What just happened? Was that real? Did they want ransom? Or worse?* I'll never know for sure, but I'm so, so thankful for my guys. (And one of them is still with me to this day.) If they hadn't been there...

I was so naive. I was young and dumb, and I'd put myself in serious danger. All for about $400 worth of shoes, though of course that is a lot of money in India.

I was so unprepared for that experience, and it made a serious impression on me. I'll never walk into another culture unprepared like that again.

Hopefully you'll never have an experience like mine, but being prepared isn't just important in an international life-or-death situation; it's essential in your everyday circumstances too. If you're going to practice grit and grind, you've got to be prepared.

Prepare Yourself

You can't help someone else be prepared if you're not prepared yourself. So start by making preparedness a priority in your own life. Being prepared shows intentionality and respect for the people in your life and the world around you. Preparedness is also how you set yourself up for success. Why do people fail to make their dreams come true? Because they don't bother to make the preparations necessary to achieve inevitable success, one challenge at a time.

Preparation is an art. It takes dedication and continually upleveling your awareness. I've found that if I practice this, my life flows more smoothly, even on the tough days.

Acknowledge Your Dreams

What do you want out of life? What are your dreams? We all had dreams as kids. We wanted to be ballerinas or doctors or Olympic athletes. Whatever happened to those dreams? For most of us, it wasn't a conscious decision. We didn't wake up one day and say, "Nope. Doctoring is not for me. Never mind." More likely, we were overwhelmed by the amount of work and preparation we would need to do to make that dream come true. So we just let it go, slowly, over time.

I think that as we grow up, we learn to stop dreaming. We think, *Oh, that will never happen. I should just stop wasting time on it.* Well, if you don't have dreams in the first place, you're right—they will never happen. And that's just plain sad, because with the right attitude and enough preparation, you can accomplish amazing things.

Do you remember when you stopped dreaming?

Or do you still dream, but just don't know how to make them come true?

As much as I've accomplished in my life already, I still have dreams… BIG dreams! I want to give back to this world that has given me so much. I want to make a difference. I want to spread my heart around the world. The important thing is that I know what my dreams are, and you should too.

And I'm not willing to just sit back and wait for my dreams to happen someday...maybe. I guarantee you that I'm out there doing what I can to make them happen. Is it going to take some grit and grind? Yes! Am I going to need to prepare? Absolutely! And I love that. Nothing worth doing is just handed to you on a silver platter.

So what do you want out of life? What are your dreams? Where do you want to go? What do you want to experience? Acknowledging your dreams is the first step to helping them come true.

Write them down somewhere. Fantasize about every aspect. How does that dream smell? What does it look like? How will you feel when it's done? Then place a visual reminder someplace you'll see every day.

Want to travel to Italy? Great! Put pictures of Rome and Venice on your phone as a screensaver. Start your preparations by learning some Italian phrases.

Want to become a doctor? Find a picture of a diploma from the university of your choice, print it out, and post it on your refrigerator—maybe even Photoshop your name into it. And do some research into what tests you have to pass to qualify for admission.

Some may call it visualizing or magical thinking, but I just consider it good preparation. Assume the best is going to happen eventually, and then prepare for it.

Set Your Goals

One of the problems with dreams is that they can seem so far away that we'll never get there. For so many people, life just happens TO them. They don't take active control of their experiences. What is the point of that? Yes, it's great to be able to roll with the punches and be flexible. I have to think on my feet all the time. I have to pivot when the circumstances warrant it. But there's a big difference between being adaptable and being apathetic.

If you want to see your dreams happen, you have to have measurable goals. What separates dreamers from doers is the ability to take an abstract idea out of the mind and put it into concrete steps that will lead to a successful outcome.

Who do you think will actually get to Italy? Someone who dreams about it all day long and says, "Maybe...someday...I'll have the money to go"? Or the person who makes up an itinerary, researches lodging, decides what they'll do when they get to each city they plan to visit, studies the language, and looks up airline ticket prices? Notice I didn't say to buy a ticket. Maybe that's not in the cards yet. It's okay. You're still preparing for ultimate success. Those are all concrete steps that don't cost anything but time and energy. The person who goes through all that preparation has made the switch from dreaming about a plan to actually implementing it.

So take those dreams you wrote down just a moment ago and reverse engineer your success by breaking them down into smaller, actionable goals you can achieve.

Let's say you want to bring all your friends or family together for a big party. You don't see each other enough, and sometimes people just need a reason to get together. This is something I do with my girlfriends at Christmas time, and it's so important to me that this year I started planning it months in advance. When they received their invitations last January, my girlfriends thought I was crazy. They teased me mercilessly about it at first. "There goes Rhonda!" and "She's planning everything Rhonda-style!"

Yet planning that far in advance accomplishes two things. First, it gives my friends enough time and space in their busy schedules to make it a priority. They may tease me about it, but most of them make arrangements to come right away. By the time the Christmas season rolls around, they appreciate the fact that someone else was willing to do the groundwork to get everyone together and make beautiful memories.

Second, it gives me the time and space to go high-touch and take care of the planning and execution of the event myself. Instead of scrambling around at the last minute, settling decorations and food and arranging for a venue, I can just enjoy the event knowing that the details are taken care of and that the most important thing has been accomplished—everyone will be together.

One recent theme for my event was the Girlfriends Gown Gala. All that was required to get in to the venue was a gown and a smile. It was special and fun, and it allowed me to give the gift of experience. We'll remember that night for years to come. Is it a lot of work? Yes. But it's worth it. So I plan ahead, because it's important to me and I care about others.

Sit down with your dreams and prepare your goals. Ask yourself, "What steps can I take this year to achieve my dream?" Then keep breaking it down further. "What steps can I take this month? This week? Today?"

Here's how the party-planning dream might look:

- **ONE YEAR IN ADVANCE:** Book a venue and order invitations.

- **ELEVEN MONTHS IN ADVANCE:** Address and mail invitations.

- **TEN MONTHS IN ADVANCE:** Choose a caterer and set the menu. Start collecting RSVPs and save them in a set location.

- **NINE MONTHS IN ADVANCE:** Interview and book musicians.

- **EIGHT MONTHS IN ADVANCE:** Plan the decorations and reserve any additional tables, chairs, or tableware needed.

- **SIX MONTHS IN ADVANCE:** Purchase decorations. Make sure you have a team in place to help decorate the venue.

- **TWO TO FOUR MONTHS IN ADVANCE:** Purchase your outfit for the event and book any appointments you'll need for hair, nails, or makeup.

- **THREE TO FOUR WEEKS BEFORE PARTY:** Double check with venue, caterer, and musicians to make sure deposits are paid and any last-minute details are taken care of.

- **WEEK OF THE PARTY:** Give the caterer the final headcount. Attend personal appointments. Set up for the event.

- **DAY OF THE PARTY:** Rely on your training!

Will unexpected things pop up from time to time? Yes. But the overall dream seems much more doable when you attach some smaller, achievable goals.

Expect Challenges

Being prepared doesn't always mean everything will go smoothly. That's why my next strategy is to be prepared to face challenges. Now obviously you can't always be prepared for everything all the time. Not everything is going to go just the way you planned. Things will go wrong. There will be breakdowns, detours, and reroutes. And I'm not just talking about car trouble—I'm talking about life.

Knowing that sometimes things are going to hit the fan can help you keep a cool head no matter what happens. You'll be able to adjust and adapt quickly. And when you can do that, you have an edge that others don't have. Those challenges will just be another opportunity to practice your grit and grind with a smile.

So how can you prepare for unforeseen challenges? After all, you don't know what to expect until they arise. All you can do is think ahead to what could possibly happen. Run scenarios in your head—bad ones and catastrophic ones.

You're at a train station in Italy and find you've lost your passport. Crap! What would you do? Well, thankfully you were smart and packed a photocopy in your wallet. So you can use that until you can get to the consulate and order a new one.

Thank goodness you considered that scenario ahead of time, because now you know two things. One, it's a really good idea to photocopy your passport, just in case. And two, you should probably know the location of the American consulate and maybe even familiarize yourself with how to get a replacement passport overseas.

Now, there is a real danger of getting caught in a negative loop here. Sometimes thinking about challenges can make us feel like the dream is unachievable or a really bad idea. ("No thanks, I've decided that trip to Cabo isn't for me. What if I go snorkeling and get eaten by a shark!") So remember, you're preparing for things that might happen. More than likely, those scenarios will never come up. But just the fact that you successfully solved the lost-passport kerfuffle in your mind means that you can more confidently handle whatever real situations actually do arise.

Before you walk into a situation, take a moment (or two) to run through a few contingencies. For instance, let's say you get a memo that the department head wants to meet with you first thing tomorrow morning. There's no indication what the meeting will be about, but you want to be ready for whatever might come up. You've been in meetings with him before and know he likes to ask questions about key metrics and assignment benchmarks. As you leave the office that evening, you grab a thumb drive and download the files you'll need to brush up on the assignment's performance thus far. You'll be ready. Whether it's personal or work, it's much easier to face things head-on if you can see them coming and prepare yourself.

Take Risks

I'm the first to admit that I'm a risk-taker, but I've learned to go in with my eyes open. I don't jump into things, especially not dangerous situations, without doing my homework first. It's important to assess risks in terms of what they might gain for you in the long run. We'll discuss that more in just a minute. But for now, realize that risks can be mitigated with proper preparation.

Be prepared for the Universe (or God, if you prefer) to tap you in different ways. Sometimes you'll be asked to do things you don't feel you're ready for. Learn to recognize those taps, assess the risk, and— if you feel in your gut that it's the right thing to do—go all-in.

Learning to trust your gut is a skill that's perfected over time. The more risks you take that turn out fine, the more confidence you'll have the next time. I go with my gut a lot. There's a rhythm and cadence that you just feel when everything is in sync. That's when you can play full out without being afraid. Some things I've done or opportunities I've followed didn't look like good ideas on the surface. But I've been able to go into them full contact by being prepared, knowing who I was and what I could do, and recognizing what the end goals were.

About 10 years ago, an opportunity came up for my team to go to London on a three-year assignment. My husband and I had just gotten engaged. It would have been easy to turn the job down because it meant some major adjustments in my life. But I recognized the tap. I thought, *I really need to take this*. It was going to be a challenge, and a huge part of me didn't want to go. Still, I felt the Universe tapping on my shoulder and whispering in my ear, "Take a chance."

So I did. I took the job and made it work.

It wasn't easy. I had to take a 6-hour flight home every Friday after work to spend 48 hours with my family, then fly back at 6 pm Sunday night in order to get to work in time on Monday morning. I went to work straight from the airport. It was brutal. But I did it—I gritted it out. And I'm glad I did. I was able to make a huge difference in that company and for countless people whose lives were tied up in it.

Be Willing to Sacrifice for the Long Game

Sometimes you have to do things you don't want to do. It's not called grit and grind for nothing. Think about when you were a kid. Did you love brushing your teeth twice a day? Probably not. Did you do it anyway? Yeah, because your mom made you. But I bet it wasn't very fun for her either. So why did she keep insisting? If you weren't enjoying it and she wasn't enjoying it, why not just let everyone off the hook?

Your mother was willing to endure the endless reminders and your reluctant sighs because, in the long run, she wanted you to have teeth. She recognized that it was a short-term pain for a long-term gain, so she was prepared to take whatever steps necessary to make sure you kept up your dental hygiene. If you enjoy having teeth right now, go call your mother and say thanks.

Learn how to recognize those necessary moments where your short-term sacrifice will be worth the long-term benefit. Be ready for them. Take the off-chance opportunities that come your way. They can pay off in a big way down the line.

Not everybody will be willing to take the short-term risk. Most people won't even acknowledge to themselves that they recognized the opportunity. Don't play blindly like that. Don't fool yourself. Yes, there may be parts of it you won't like, things you don't enjoy doing. But they may lead to bigger and better things down the line.

You Can't ALWAYS Be Prepared... and That's Okay

As much as I'd like to think that a person can prepare for anything, I know that's not true. If anyone could, it would be me. I have preparation down to an art, because I have to in my line of work. But I readily admit that there are some things you just can't prepare for, and you won't know what they are until you're right in the middle of the mess. But it's not all bad. Sometimes, you're not prepared for how amazing an ordinary experience will turn out to be. When you're alert and aware of what's going on around you, surprises can make life richer and so much more rewarding.

In August 2018, my best friend Michelle and I went to South Africa on a trip we'd been planning for over a year. It was a birthday trip for us both, and we were excited to go on safari and see the wildlife. I've traveled all over the world, and I did my usual brushing up on the current events and culture. It seemed like it was going to be a pretty low-key, fun trip. I'd been to South Africa before for work, but I wasn't mentally prepared for THIS Africa. I was completely blindsided by how much the people there affected me spiritually. I was so moved by their strength, resilience, and beauty.

Two things that happened during the trip left a mark on my life I know will last forever. The first was the children. While I was there, I went to a community children's school and watched them learning English. I had the chance to show them modern technology for the first time. Then I visited a local Maasai tribe and had a chance to visit the tribal chief's son. He let us into his home and allowed us to sit for an hour in his cow-dung house.

When I got back home to the States, one of the first things I did was ship them tons of water along with framed photos of my best friend and me with the chief's son. And do you know what? They sent me back pictures of themselves with all the water. This resource is a treasure to them because the women go out and walk miles for water every day. Their smiles were so infectious. That's real. They're part of my heart now.

The other thing that made a huge impact on me while I was there was something I usually take for granted—running. As I described earlier in this chapter, I was training for an upcoming race, and I'm serious about my training, even while I'm traveling. I plan my races a year in advance, and the South Africa trip fell right in the middle of my training for the Eagleman 70.3-mile triathlon. I knew I needed to come up with a plan that would allow me to keep training while I was there so I could be ready and prepared for the race, which was just 48 hours after I landed back in the States. That meant I was going to need to run across the Serengeti. No big deal, right?

Except apparently it is a big deal. People thought I was crazy at the resort when I announced that I wanted to go for a training run across the 350,000-acre Singita Grumeti Reserve. I wasn't aware that the Serengeti can be really dangerous, between the wild animals and the poachers. Just the week before, one of the park rangers had been charged by a water buffalo and had landed in the hospital. It would have been easier to just stay in or hit the treadmill. Wild animals like lions and water buffalo roam freely, and poachers are always lurking around. But I was committed to running outside (I HATE the treadmill), so I knew was going to have to get creative in order to be prepared.

And that ended up with me running alongside four armed guards in a Jeep—the amazing staff at the Singita resort insisted on it for my protection—setting off across the Serengeti. It must have been a really strange sight—one white woman running through the savannah with a small convoy of armed soldiers.

The next day, all these men who worked at the resort were waiting when I came out to run. They wanted to run with me too, and so did some local women and children. So we all ran together.

Unexpectedly, that run sparked a moment that's become a partner-ship for a yearly event with the BRAVE-Singita Grumeti Fund for the All-Women Run Across the Serengeti, a 5-day, 55-mile run that raises money for the Singita Grumeti Fund for Women's Empowerment. Doing the All-Women Run Across the Serengeti, being there with the beautiful people who have become my dear friends, and making connections with women and children across the globe impacted me profoundly. There's no way I could have foreseen such a wonder-ful event coming out of my simple need to go for a run.

Had I not taken the short-term risk, braving the lions and buffalo and the heat and the poachers, I'd have completely missed the op-portunity to get involved with a project that has come to mean the world to me. I would not have made such deep, lasting connections with people like Khalid and Edward, and my bodyguard Helen, who I bonded closely with. And I wouldn't have had the time of my life running across the Serengeti with other amazing women and girls who I love and admire so much. My world is bigger—and smaller—than it was before I left on that birthday trip. And I know I'm a better person for the experience.

The Price of NOT Being Prepared

There are certain things in life you can just get by on. You can float your way through and fly by the seat of your pants. Want my advice on that?

Don't.

For one thing, do you really want that to be the legacy you leave? Do you want to be known as the person who was always "wing-ing it"? Plus, (and deep down you know this), the really worthwhile things in life are the ones that require more preparation, not less. It's nice to have the confidence to wing it when you need to. But it's also amazing to have the discipline to prepare ahead of time and practically guarantee a successful outcome.

As I've mentioned, I run Ironman races. Training for them is my personal time—the time I use to think, plan, and strategize. I spend hours upon hours training every week, so I can say this without a shred of hesitation. You can't complete a triathlon without training. I mean you can't. It doesn't work.

Oh, you could say, "I'm going to run a race! I know how to bike, and I know how to swim, and I can sort of run. It'll be fine!" A lot of people do that. They underestimate the level of strength and stamina they'll need. They're not prepared, and sometimes they end up doing themselves permanent damage.

The first 70.3-mile Ironman I ever did was in Cambridge, Maryland, in 2017. You could pick out the people who weren't prepared right away. They thought they could just go out and do it. Or maybe they did a little training, but not a lot. It was a disaster for them. They weren't prepared for the difficulty of the course or the six-foot swells they would have to swim through, and they ended up in the hospital.

Yes, it takes a lot of time. And it takes a lot of energy. In the weeks before a race, I run for an hour and fifteen minutes every day and train four hours on the weekends. People think I'm crazy when I tell them I have to sleep and I have to eat. "Why do you need to sleep, like why are you in bed Sunday at 4:30 pm?" Because I have to get up and train in the wee hours of the morning. Because I want to be as prepared as I possibly can. Because I want a successful outcome.

It's the race. It's what I love. I make the sacrifices to prepare well because I want to do my best. I don't let myself make excuses. The one I hear most often is "I don't have time." Sure you do! Schedule it like you would a meeting. Put the race on the calendar, then schedule out training from there.

You can do that with any big goal or task. Whether that's cooking a Thanksgiving dinner for your in-laws or making a big pitch to a venture capital firm for start-up funding. Schedule it out, then plan it back. Break it up so it's doable, then dive in. You can do it!

Prepare YOUR TEAM

When you know how to prepare yourself for success, it's much easier to transfer those skills over to your team. We all lead teams in life—whether it's made up of tens of thousands of employees all over the world, your local church group, your family, or on the sports field. At some point, you'll be asked to lead someone somewhere. And the more often you do that successfully, the more often you'll be asked to lead bigger teams to bigger outcomes.

I started out leading small local technology teams, and a few quick decades later, I now handle a team of over 100,000 people all over the world.

Big or small, the team you're leading depends on you, which means you need to take on the burden of responsibility. If the team fails, it means YOU failed. You failed to achieve the outcome, and you failed as a leader. Once you realize that, you start to take preparation really seriously.

One of the most humiliating experiences of my life was standing face-to-face with the CEO of a company I'd just taken on, and being screamed at for not being ready with a five-year plan I didn't even know he wanted.

I was three months into a new position and had inherited a team that had already been in place with that corporation for some time. We had just gone into a strategy session that no one had prepped for. We were completely, totally unprepared. I didn't know we were expected to have a five-year plan ready to present.

When you go from being prepared as an individual to being prepared as a team, there's more on the line. If you fail to prepare your team, not only do you look sloppy, everyone else does too. If you're in a position of leadership, you absolutely must take steps to make sure your team is prepared no matter what. Here are the steps I take to make sure my team and I are prepared.

KNOW THE MATERIAL

At least 48 hours before I walk into a meeting, I always ask for any materials that will be covered. This gives me time to get familiar with what will be discussed without having to listen to someone read off a slide deck. I hate that. It's honestly one of my pet peeves.

KNOW THE AGENDA

What exactly will be covered? And what outcomes are expected? When I walked into the meeting I mentioned above, I didn't know what the corporation's future strategy was. I assumed that because they were an established, well-known entity, they had a good business strategy. That was a mistake. The CEO was looking for a new five-year plan, and I had no idea that was the agenda for the meeting. No one had warned us.

And speaking of strategy, don't assume an idea is a good one until you've bounced it off a couple of relevant people. Find out what the company's goals and objectives are before presenting them with a plan that may or may not work in that culture.

DO PRACTICE RUNS

Before my team and I go into an important meeting or presentation, I do dry runs with them. We will practice the whole thing from top to bottom. We role play, conduct question and answer sessions, you name it. By the time we walk into that meeting, my team knows the material top to bottom. They know what to say, how to say it—

everything right down to where they should stand. And we walk in with our heads held high because we know we're ready. We have every right to be confident.

SCHEDULE BACKWARD

I hate Friday fire drills. What do I mean by that? When things go sideways at the last minute and no one's prepared, people panic. To avoid that, I make sure we're ready WAY ahead of time. When I know there's a big meeting coming up, I back up the deadlines for the whole team about three weeks.

I make sure my team has clear goals and deliverables and that they know what's expected of them. This is their race, and they can't just wing it. There's a certain cadence to working with me, and it involves lots of advance preparation. They know that. They're prepared for it. So we all win big!

Prepare for the CULTURE and WORLD Around You

I was so unprepared when I went to India in my twenties. I was young and naive back then. I didn't know anything about the culture. I didn't dress appropriately or take precautions to keep myself safe. I didn't respect the customs and people around me. And I could have paid for it with my life. It was a hard but important lesson to learn. It doesn't take a lot to prepare myself when I know I'll be interacting with a new audience or culture, either in another part of the world or at home. It's just a matter of doing a little homework ahead of time.

Before I set foot on a plane or walk into a boardroom full of professionals from another culture, I do my homework. Keep in mind, culture doesn't necessarily mean another country. There are countless unique cultures right here in the States. Golf is another culture.

New York City and Boston are both very different cultures I have to navigate regularly. Even if you're not travelling internationally or interacting with people from another country, you may still be dealing with another culture. And for that, you must be prepared.

DRESS FOR THE CULTURE

When you're engaging with people from another culture, find common ground so you can open up communication and foster a sense of connection. An easy way to start, especially when traveling overseas, is by simply dressing like they do. When I'm in India now, I wear saris everywhere—I own more than 70. I dress not only to blend in, but also to show respect for their culture and to honor their practices. When I'm in the Middle East, I do wear a burka when I'm traveling outdoors between meetings. It's more than just a safety thing. It's a respect thing too. Had I been wearing a sari when I was nearly kidnapped in India all those years ago, the whole thing might never have occurred.

MIND YOUR MANNERISMS

This one is easy to overlook because we often take for granted the body language and mannerisms we use in our own homes. Gestures that mean one thing here can mean something entirely different to another culture, so not looking into the mannerisms of the other culture is a big mistake.

Take a simple handshake, for example. Here in the States, it's a mere formality. A handshake is great, but it's just kind of the default greeting that can easily be replaced with a high five or fist bump. In Asian cultures, treating the handshake as a throwaway gesture is extremely insulting. If you don't give a genuine, heartfelt handshake complete with eye contact and slight bow, you're seen as disrespectful, and you'll have a hard time convincing that person to work with you.

KEEP TABS ON THE NEWS

Pick up a newspaper before you get on an airplane and read the current events for the place you're going. I always check the news before I travel. I know what I'm diving into before I get on a plane. I won't hesitate to go full contact into a situation, but I won't go in blindly if I can help it.

BE AWARE OF SECURITY ISSUES

I learned so much from my experience in India. I am always on alert when I'm away from home. I'm always aware of my surroundings. My position dictates that I not go places alone, and I have guards now who stay with me all the time. That time in India, I put myself in a position where I stood out from the crowd. Then I made it even more dangerous by shopping alone. In other countries, like Korea or Singapore, an attempted kidnapping like that would never happen. But I didn't know, because I didn't do my homework.

I could have quit after my kidnapping experience in India. I think most people would have, right? They'd have hopped on a plane and gone home. I didn't—but I also didn't keep doing things the way I was doing them. I was in India for a long time back and forth, and I learned how to embed myself in the culture. Sensible Rhonda kicked in, and I did what I needed to do to be safe and feel secure there again. I learned the culture and how to navigate it, and it made all the difference for me. Eventually, I became the first female to insource people over in India for a major multinational financial corporation. That made a difference to thousands of families in both countries, and I'm so grateful to have played a part. I still have many friends there.

The Key to Preparation

If you feel like you're struggling to keep up and always flying by the seat of your pants, it's time to put the brakes on. Sit down with your schedule and do an honest assessment, keeping one key thing in mind...

Saying yes to one thing means you're saying no to something else.

Being prepared is a balancing act. And the first step is taking control of your schedule now so you can build the time and preparation into your life and accomplish the things that are really important. It might not be easy. But it's all part of the grit and grind.

FOCUS STATEMENT
*I am prepared
and ready for anything.*

2

SHOW RESPECT
Or Show Yourself Out

There's a special section of my closet where I love spending time. The garments hanging there range in hue from rich, vibrant jewel tones to basic black in beaded and sequined satin all the way to practical, breathable cotton. But it's not the colors or the fabrics that draws me to them. It's the experiences they represent.

When I first started traveling internationally for work, I dressed like any professional American business woman would. I wanted to be taken seriously, and I packed what I thought would portray strength, respect, and intelligence. Although my power suits and polished appearance were definitely professional, I wasn't achieving the effect I was looking for.

I was acknowledged. I was treated politely. But in boardrooms across the globe I could tell there was something missing in my interactions. Executives in other countries just weren't relating to me the way I had hoped. I wanted these executives to know how deeply I respected them and the businesses they ran, but I was falling short in conveying it.

It wasn't until I stopped wearing plain clothes when I traveled in India and started wearing traditional Indian saris, even when I was in boardrooms and conference centers, that something interesting happened. My relationship with the executives I met with grew considerably warmer. That's when the light bulb went on. I had been showing up in my suit and heels and expecting them to show me respect on my own terms. That might work in the States, but in many other countries around the world, it falls flat.

Respect is not a given. If you want respect, you must show it first. I had unknowingly been alienating myself from the very people I wanted so badly to connect with, by showing up and expecting them to adjust to me. When I began wearing the traditional clothing of the country I was in, I was showing respect for the executives I was meeting with. They could see my interest in their culture and customs just by looking at me.

So simple. So easy. Today when I travel, I always dress according to the country I'm in. Saris in India, burkas in the Middle East. I've even donned traditional Korean ceremonial clothing on occasion to visit remote villages in South Korea.

Respect, even in the small things you and I might find insignificant, can mean the world to someone in another culture. But before you can respect someone in another culture, you have to learn to respect someone else even closer to home.

You.

Respect Yourself

On a scale from 1 to 10, how well do you think you respect yourself? Have you ever considered that?

Sure I respect myself. Of course. Who doesn't?

Truthfully, a lot of people don't. I think lack of self-respect is like an epidemic in our society. It's trendy in the corporate world to work too much, sleep too little, have a poor diet, and neglect the people you love. It's an unusual executive or entrepreneur who doesn't live like that, and I'm not okay with it. It's not healthy or sustainable. Trust me, I've lived it.

When I was younger, I worked far too many hours. It seemed like it was just par for the course—until I found myself crashing every weekend and sleeping 13 hours at a time. I couldn't keep going like that. It just didn't work for me. I knew that meant I was going to have to make some changes, and change is hard. Respecting yourself is hard. If you don't find a way to do it though, you'll never be able to really get a good handle on respecting others.

RESPECT YOUR PHYSICAL HEALTH

Don't let your health go by the wayside because you think you have to work 24/7. If you're not keeping yourself physically fit, how will you manage a team or serve your family? Not everyone has to train for Ironman Triathlons, but find something you do love doing that's good for you, and invest in it. I plan my schedule around my training. Knowing I have time built into my day to take care of myself helps me to manage stress. And I find that I have more clarity in decision making when I incorporate fitness into my days.

RESPECT YOUR MENTAL AND EMOTIONAL HEALTH

Being a corporate executive can eat away at every single minute of your life. So can being an entrepreneur or a parent or a customer service provider. Life has the potential to run you over if you let it. It's important to treat yourself with kindness. Remember, you set the tone for how others respect you.

Your mind and emotions can get confused. A healthy mental state means you're able to accurately process information and behave accordingly. A healthy emotional state means you're comfortable expressing your feelings without fear. Both require you to give yourself a break when things go sideways in your life.

I believe in diving right into the grit and grind and going full contact with everything I do. But you've got to keep things in perspective. Expecting perfection isn't realistic, and you're setting yourself up for huge levels of stress and disappointment if you put that kind of weight on yourself. Treat yourself like you would treat a beloved child. Cut yourself some slack as you're learning. Grit and grind is a practice, remember? Protect your mental and emotional health by using failures and challenges to help you grow. Your brain will be happy to let you take more chances when it knows you're not going to chastise yourself if things don't turn out as expected.

Respecting yourself is just the first step, but it's the most important one. When you care for and honor yourself and your needs, you model that to others around you. People can read it through your actions, and it makes an impression.

Respect Your Team

Everyone needs a team. No man is an island, and you can accomplish exponentially more as a team than you can as an individual. Your team can be made up of your staff and coworkers, your friends and family, or a combination of the two. I have teams in multiple areas of my life, depending on the situation and circumstances I'm in. I have my own work team that accompanies me on jobs wherever I go. I also manage teams of up to hundreds of thousands through the corporations I serve. Then I have several very tight-knit groups of people in my home and personal life that I consider my nucleus.

Regardless of who they are or what area of your life they're in, your team is the ones you go to battle with and the people who have your back. They "have your six" as my military friends say. They'll stand in the gap for you when you fall short and celebrate with you when you win. They're the ones who come running when you send out an SOS and the ones who are in the trenches with you every day. I cannot overemphasize how important your teams are.

My web developer, Katherine, had a problem. When I hired her to create my website, she had two other large projects going on. My website was a large project too, larger than we all originally thought it would be, and when I spoke with her, I could tell she was underwater. Being a freelancer can be tough. Every client you have wants to think they're your top priority—they may not care that you have other clients and projects going on at the same time. I knew she must be trying really hard to keep everyone happy.

No, the website wasn't done as soon as we thought it would be, but my gut told me she was the right person for the job. I had a choice to make. I could choose to make this a miserable experience for her—and for me—by pressuring and demanding results faster. We both would have come out of the project unhappy and probably would never have worked together again.

But that kind of atmosphere doesn't help anyone. I know that as the person in the client/employer role, I set the tone for our working relationship. I had taken her on as part of my team for that project, and to me that means she's part of the family. I decided to do whatever I could to make this a positive experience that valued her as a person and celebrated her skills, regardless of the time frame.

It doesn't matter who your team is—you have a choice about how you treat them. People will work harder and produce better work when they feel valued and appreciated. When you stay positive and come alongside your team, the atmosphere is lighter, healthier, and more productive. By all means, push those projects to the finish line. But be a leader, not a dictator. Push right alongside your team with kindness and positivity. Then when the project or task is finished, you can all celebrate together. That's respect. If you want your team to respect you, you need to demonstrate respect for them. You've got to go back to the basics.

TREAT OTHERS HOW YOU WANT TO BE TREATED. This principle is simple, but not always easy. How you treat others is how they will treat you. It might not happen overnight, but it will come back to you.

WALK THE WALK. You know that old saying "Do as I say, not as I do"? Just take that phrase right out of your vocabulary. Walk the walk before you talk the talk. Show your team by example what you expect in return. Work alongside them. Live alongside them. Laugh and play alongside them. It will 100% improve the culture of your team.

BE PRESENT. There's a big difference between working FOR someone and working WITH them. Be the kind of person who works with people. Show up. Be accessible. My job as a leader is to take care of the team, but I can't do that if I'm not spending time with them or if they can't reach me when they need me. There are things you'll never see and won't have the chance to address if you're not plugged in to what's going on with your team. I always say I work for the team.

HELP THEM BE PREPARED. It's my job to make sure the teams are trained well and given the tools and skills they need to succeed and represent their company well. But how will I know if there's a gap in their learning if I don't spend time with them? I've been known to go to rather extreme lengths to make sure my teams are trained well, even in the small things.

One example of this is the time I brought in an expert to train a team on dining room etiquette. The teams spend a lot of time in formal dining situations with other CEOs and executives, and I noticed that many had no grasp of the proper etiquette. I wanted them to represent the company well, so the expert gave a detailed presentation. Afterward, we sat down to a complete multicourse meal on formal place settings. What they didn't know was that the expert and I were watching and assessing them during the meal.

After dinner, I gave them their "grades." It was fun and meaningful, and it made a memorable impression. I spent extra time and energy preparing the exercise for my team because I wanted them to be the best they can be.

I value them so highly, and I make sure they know it. The way I see it is I work for them, not the other way around. I want my team to walk away from interactions with me feeling positive and energized. In the technology field, respect often isn't a key metric. Productivity is prioritized above people. I'm all for productivity. It's one of the things my team prides itself on. But I never let it take precedence over kindness.

Pay Attention

Don't be afraid to immerse yourself in new cultures. Our world is big, and it deserves to be explored and learned from. Be open to change and new experiences, because those are the things that will make you a more global leader. I take any chance I can get to bond with people while I'm overseas. Who knows when those opportunities will ever present themselves again?

Whenever I'm traveling for work, I always take a half day to go somewhere with my team that will give them a cultural experience. We visited the Taj Mahal in India, the Kremlin in Russia, the Great Wall of China, Big Ben in London. Those experiences help connect the team with the different cultures we serve. Sometimes those experiences change your life.

I had a life-changing experience like that when I was in India several years ago. It came to my attention that the corporation I was working with supported some community outreach programs, one of which was a local orphanage. The facility was run by nuns and was home to children with no parents and children whose parents had abandoned or surrendered them to the state because they couldn't care for them. I knew I needed to go visit that orphanage.

I wasn't prepared for the impact that dozens of children without homes and parents would have on me. We were strangers to them, yet they were so happy to see us and invite us into their lives. We sat down on the floor with them and played together, and none of our differences mattered. We didn't speak the same language. We didn't have the same skin color. The circumstances those children had lived through...I couldn't imagine. Yet we connected, and it broke my heart and changed me.

I go back to visit that orphanage every time I'm in India. When we go, we ship clothes, diapers, toys, chocolate, and school supplies ahead of us to deliver to the children. One year, we even brought them one of those motorized cars they could sit in and "drive." I just want to bring a smile to those kids' faces. I want them to know that someone on the other side of the world sees them, is thinking about them, and is respectfully caring for them in a way that's acceptable in their culture.

The thing is, if you're not paying attention to what's going on around you, you'll miss out on opportunities to really immerse yourself in the culture. Yes, it was a sacrifice to make time to visit the orphanage that day. We were tired. We had lots of work to catch up on. We had a full schedule of meetings every day. But I would never trade that experience for the world, and neither would anyone else on the team. I remember one gentleman on the team, Rick, saying to me, "This is the best birthday present ever," because we had visited on his birthday.

Full-Contact Respect

How will respect help you with the grit and grind of daily life? How will it help you succeed? It makes you a person worth listening to. It shows people they can trust you. I've seen leaders come and go, people in positions of power all over the world. Disrespect has always been a major contributor to their downfall. Fortunately, we all have a choice. When you purposely infuse respect into everything you do, you will reap the rewards.

FOCUS STATEMENT

I respect myself, my team,
and the world around me.

3

BE ON TIME

Time Lies...I Mean Flies

I first became friends with Laurie when we worked together in technology. She was an executive in a company I worked with, and she really was a technical genius. But deep down at her core, she was a talented musician, which I found fascinating.

I'll never forget our first meeting together. I walked into the room, and right away I noticed the synthesizer and amp in the corner. During the first part of the meeting, I watched to see if I could pinpoint who the musician was. It didn't take long to pick her out.

There's something uniquely special about musicians. Former and current members of the military are the same. They have an innate timing, a cadence that I really work well with. Laurie had that something. When there was a lull in the meeting, I didn't waste time asking her if she would play something for us, and it became a favorite part of our meetings together. She operated at her highest level as an executive when she could tap into her musicality. It brought an amazing rhythm and meter to her work that I still admire to this day.

Not all musicians—or all people, for that matter—respect time like she does. Take the drummer in the band Laurie was in. He was so talented, but although he had all the rhythm in the world musically, he couldn't get to a gig on time to save his life. He was the stereotypical drummer who always had a sexy woman on his arm and was too cool to be on time.

That would never fly on my watch.

Time is the only truly nonrenewable resource. Undervaluing other people's time—or your own—is wasteful and, frankly, disrespectful. You can make more money. You can buy more things. But time isn't like that. You can't just go out and buy or make it somehow. There's no time factory, no manufactured minutes, no store that sells seconds. Each person gets 1,440 minutes every day. Period. How you use the time you have MATTERS.

Fudging a few minutes here and there doesn't seem like a big deal at first. But if you want to live a full-contact life and fully invest in your goals and aspirations, being on time must be a priority. The consequences—both physical and emotional—of not being on time are even more costly to you than the loss of your time itself.

Tiny Little Lateness Lies

So many people don't take being on time seriously. They think they're fine. "Oh, I'm only five minutes late." Or "It's fashionable to be late." "It's not a big deal." "I'm not really a late person." Let me tell you right now, you're lying to yourself. Not valuing time is a problem. And the root causes of that problem are the lies we tell ourselves about lateness.

- I think I'm on time...most of the time.

- A few minutes late isn't really late.

- They won't care if I'm a little late. They probably won't be there on time either.

- I'm not late THAT often.

- I've got time to do just one more thing before I go.

Do any of those sound familiar? If they do, then you're buying into the lie of lateness. You're listening to the falsehood that it doesn't matter if you're on time and it won't make a difference if you're a little late. Let me tell you—it matters.

If the statements above have a familiar ring to them, I have a challenge for you. It's pretty quick and easy—just three steps—but it will help you determine whether you have a problem with lateness. It's also an effective way to pinpoint the things that are keeping you from being on time. All you need for this challenge is a notebook or even the notepad app on your phone to record what you find.

STEP 1: Check the time when you actually arrive somewhere. I don't mean make a guesstimate or give a ballpark figure. I want you to note the exact time.

STEP 2: Were you on time? Three minutes late? Twenty minutes late? Calculate how late you were.

STEP 3: When you're late, ask yourself why. Look for patterns in your behavior and thoughts. Did you underestimate the traffic? Were you trying to finish up a few little things before you left? Did others interrupt your routine with their needs at the wrong time? Evaluate how you're using and thinking about your time so you can pinpoint where your time leaks are and take steps to repair them.

Don't buy into the lie of lateness. Do the work now to get back on track. It's not too late to form a new habit, and it's so worth it. I'm going to show you some simple strategies for handling lateness, but first, let's talk about WHY being on time matters.

Being Late Shows Disrespect for Others

Time is a currency just like money, but unlike money, you can't make more. Once you spend it, it's gone forever. Imagine you have a bag full of 1,440 shiny silver tokens—that's how many minutes you have every day. (And not to get too morbid here, but you really don't know if you're going to get another bag tomorrow.) So how are you going to spend those tokens?

A good 600 of them are already allocated for work and your commute. And how long do you sleep? Hand over at least another 500 of your silver pieces. How much does that leave you with today? 340. Whoa! That's not a lot of time left. Like to exercise for an hour? You have 280 left. Do you have a date tonight? Okay, 100 left. And let's not forget all the little things that take time like showering, getting dressed, managing housework, arguing with your spouse, getting kids ready for school, and scrolling through social media.

Are you starting to get the point? Time is currency.

Now, with that thought in mind, imagine you're attending a meeting or a luncheon and someone is ten minutes late. Ten silver pieces are immediately deducted from everyone there. They didn't choose to spend those ten tokens, but they disappeared anyway because someone else was late. How would that make you feel? And how would you feel if you were the one causing everyone to lose a precious resource?

When you're late, it's disrespectful. Period. It's disrespectful to the world around you. It's disrespectful to your team. It's even disrespectful to yourself, because you're not valuing your own time, one of the most precious resources you have. Being late might not seem like a big deal. It's not hurting anyone, right? It's just a few minutes. But let's really break it down and consider what habitual lateness communicates to others.

- This wasn't important enough for me to make the effort to be on time.

- I value whatever I was doing before this more than I value you.

- My schedule takes precedence over yours.

- I have no control over my schedule or my life.

- I can't be trusted to show up when I say I will.

- You can't count on me to do what I say I will do.

- I don't care.

Let that sink in a little bit. Others may not come out and say something like that to your face, but that's what you're telling them when you're constantly late. And just as respect breeds respect, disrespect breeds disrespect.

I have worked with people who are habitually late, and I don't mean occasionally or just a little bit. One man in particular was late all the time. It didn't matter what the occasion was—a meeting, an event, a workout session—he was late for it. You could just plan on it. His lateness affected everyone he interacted with. The more meetings he showed up late for, the more we felt disrespected. It was as if he didn't value the team and had no stake in the project we were working on.

Eventually, we all learned to just go on without him, and he ended up missing out on a lot of important information. It got so bad that everyone got tired of pulling his weight. We felt so disrespected by his lack of concern for our time that little by little, we lost respect for him as well. I started asking him to sing nursery rhymes every time he was late. Imagine a grown man singing, "I'm a Little Teacup."

Being Late Shows Disrespect for Yourself

Think about how you feel when you're late. Imagine you're running behind on your way to a meeting—maybe it's for work, maybe it's the PTA. Your pulse speeds up a little as you glance at the time. How late am I going to be? You try to calculate the time in your head. Can I sneak in the back? Maybe no one will notice. You swallow hard as you realize you're going to be more than 15 minutes late. The meeting will have started without you, and the supplies they need for the meeting are with you in the back seat of the car. So much for sneaking in unnoticed.

Then the unthinkable happens. You see the flashing lights behind you and feel a sinking in your stomach as you glance down at the speedometer. Fifteen miles over the limit. Yikes! In your haste to get there as soon as you could and mitigate the damages your tardiness would cause, you've now made it even worse. With a frustrated sigh, you flip your blinker and pull over to the side of the road, internally chastising yourself while punching the automatic window button.

You grit your teeth, paste on a fake smile, and turn to the officer as he approaches. "Good afternoon, Officer. Was I speeding?"

When you're late, you feel bad. Your stomach sinks, and you feel guilty and anxious. When you do manage to show up, you rush in out of breath, apologizing profusely. It doesn't feel good, and it can put you on an emotional roller coaster that in most cases is completely preventable.

Laid Back...Or Just Don't Care?

But maybe you're one of those people who doesn't really get worked up over being late. Let me guess—you often describe yourself as "laid back" and a "go-with-the-flow" type of person. Life is drunk and disorderly, and so a person just has to learn to roll with the punches and not let it get to them, right? That might be what you tell yourself, but is it really true?

I don't think so. You know what I think? I think you've bought into the lie of lateness. I've worked with thousands of people from all over the globe and managed teams with over a hundred thousand members. And, more often than not when I meet someone who's a self-proclaimed "laid-back" soul, there's something else behind their inability to be on time. Sometimes they just don't realize how precious every minute of every day is for all of us. And sometimes it's a lack of caring and respect.

Ouch. That one stings a little, doesn't it? Even if that's not you, even if you really are just forgetful or free-spirited, the people around you won't see it that way. To others it probably looks like you just don't care.

I worked for one major multinational corporation for several years. When my team and I came on the scene, employees across the board were consistently around 40 minutes late. The CEO and the executives just put up with it because it had being going on so long they'd just grown accustomed to it. It was so bad that it wasn't unusual for them to be running meetings at 7:00 pm that were supposed to have been held at 3:00 pm. You better believe that was one of the first things my team and I addressed.

Being Late Erodes Trust

Maybe lateness isn't an issue for you. You're on the other side of the coin, and punctual is your middle name. You're the person who feels the effects of others' lateness and has to clean up the mess. How do you deal with someone who genuinely does not care if they're always late? How do you remedy that? Do you bring it up or let it slide?

This is something I have to deal with all the time. I prioritize being on time, but that doesn't mean everyone else around me does. I've even had to deal with superiors who don't show up on time.

It's frustrating for sure, and to be honest, I haven't always dealt with it very well. I don't have the best poker face all the time. But this is when Sensible Rhonda comes out, and I take a deep breath and think before I speak. It's a super effective strategy you can do anywhere. But there are times I take it beyond just taking a deep breath and praying for patience. Sometimes I use moments like these to create a coaching opportunity. One such moment involved a young reporter.

When I agreed to meet with her, I made it clear that I only had 30 minutes because I was meeting with a very busy executive afterward. I waited for 20 minutes, and then I got up and walked out. I had to. It wasn't fair to my next appointment to miss it because someone else was late. Like the old unspoken college classroom rule, 10 minutes is generally my limit, but I really wanted to give her the benefit of the doubt that day.

We ended up rescheduling, and wouldn't you know it, she was right on time for the rescheduled meeting. In fact, she contacted me ahead of time and asked what kind of Starbucks coffee I wanted. I really appreciated that. I decided to take the opportunity to make it a coachable moment. When she arrived, Starbucks in hand, I welcomed her politely, then got out my phone and opened up the calendar.

"I'm glad you're here," I said as I motioned to my phone, "but I want you to take a look at something. This is my calendar—it's full. I don't say that because I'm trying to seem important, I just want you to understand that my schedule is like this every day. Anything extra I add in is because I've made a purposeful point to make time for it. I've been looking forward to meeting you and made this appointment a priority in my day. You being late last time threw everything off, but because you were nice and polite in your emails, I was willing to reschedule. That doesn't always happen."

She was floored. No one had ever explained it to her this way before, and I could see the light-bulb moment as it happened. She'd never been told, "You can't do this. This is not what you do with executives. You're representing a big media company, and being late doesn't make a good impression." I hope this young woman went on to reassess the way she used her time and that of others. If she didn't, I have no doubt that this issue will come back to haunt her in the future.

Even if you're capable, people will not trust you with responsibilities if you can't even be on time. Lateness erodes the trust in a relationship, causing the other person to wonder, "If they can't even show up on time, how can I trust them with my project?"

Being Late Causes Opportunity Loss

Being late also indicates a lack of preparation. I've locked people out of meetings when they've showed up late, because it's so disrespectful. Everybody else is there, so where the hell were they? In the world we live in today, there are lots of other people out there who do great work. If someone can't hack it, no worries. There's always someone else out there who can. These things have a tendency to work themselves out. At some point, the person who's chronically late is going to anger and frustrate someone important, and they're going to lose out on opportunities that could have been theirs. Don't let that be you.

Even a few wasted minutes here and there add up. Minutes turn to hours, hours turn to days, days turn to weeks, and so on. Poor use of time is a major contributor to blown deadlines and missed project markers. Part of the reason I can operate with the crazy schedule I have is because I've learned to use my time well. Every day, I look at what's on my plate and assess whether or not it's something I should be investing my time into right then. Do I really want to hand over those shiny silver tokens for that particular task? Remember, saying yes to one thing means saying no to something else that might be more important or meaningful.

There's a series of questions you can ask yourself that will help bring clarity to how you spend your time. Pretend you're on your way to a committee meeting and suddenly remember you need to pick up some dry cleaning. You have a choice to make. You could get off at the next exit and pick it up before your meeting, or you could wait until after the meeting. As you consider the choices, ask yourself the following questions.

HOW MUCH TIME WILL THIS TASK REALLY TAKE? It's easy to think that a quick errand will only take a minute or two. The dry cleaner is practically on your way, and you aren't planning to come back that way later. But to get a real idea of the time a dry cleaning detour will take, you need to account for the time it takes to get to the dry cleaner's and back AND the time you'll spend completing the transaction while you're there. Depending on what time it is, maybe you can get in and out in less than five minutes, but that's during low traffic hours. During heavy traffic hours, you could be in line for 15 to 20 minutes. When all is said and done, this task could take up to half an hour.

WHO WOULD IT BENEFIT? Honestly, the only person who would benefit from this little side trip would be you.

WHAT LONG-TERM IMPACT WOULD IT HAVE ON THE MEETING? Grabbing the dry cleaning before the meeting will make you late. You'll be leaving the other committee members in limbo until you arrive, leaving them feeling off-balance and wondering where you are. Plus, if you show up 15–30 minutes late, it will take at least another 15–30 minutes to get you up to speed and back to business. You could potentially lose an hour of planning and strategy time.

DOES THIS TASK CONTRIBUTE TO THE SUCCESS OF THE PROJECT? Not in the least. Picking up your dry cleaning has nothing to do with the committee meeting.

WHY WOULD YOU DO THIS TASK? If you're being transparent, you'd only be doing this task now to save yourself time and energy later. It doesn't benefit anyone on the committee; in fact, it only takes time away from them. Perhaps there's another way. Could you ask someone else to pick it up for you? Could you combine it with a shopping trip the next day?

No matter what choices you're making between multiple ways to spend your time, make an objective assessment using these questions. You'll soon recognize the time leaks you fall prey to and the things you tend to justify to the detriment of others.

Time Leaks

Time flies. At least that's what people are so fond of saying. I don't necessarily think that's true. I think time leaks. Certain things in our lives just tend to be time wasters. They get us off our game. They siderail our progress. They steal our silver coins. Learning to recognize your time leaks is the first step to dealing with them. Do you recognize any of these?

DISTRACTIONS

The phone is going to ring, your email inbox will overflow, people do "drive-bys" and pop into your office unannounced. Distractions are unavoidable, and it's your job to deal with them. How? Let me give you a tip: accept them as par for the course. The world isn't going to stop so you can focus. So make a conscious decision about which distractions you'll tolerate and how often.

For example, I can't handle the constant notifications from Facebook. It's just not something I'm willing to put up with. But I do keep up on Twitter, Instagram, and email, because I like to stay relevant. I cut out things I know will be too distracting and interfere with my productivity while still keeping a few channels open so people can reach me.

Distractions aren't ALL bad. They can serve as a wake-up call reminding you to take a break. Sometimes you need to step away from whatever you're working on, recenter, then dive back in with renewed interest. But it's important to keep track of what's actually a distraction and whether it's something you want to tolerate or do away with. Every minute that ticks by is silver you've spent, whether you chose to or not.

THE UNEXPECTED

You can't plan for everything. Believe me, if I could, I would. But there are just some things you can't prepare for. Expect the un-expected. These things happen, and there's nothing wrong with getting thrown off-kilter. If unexpected circumstances and events freeze you and render you incapable of moving forward, you're missing an opportunity to dive into a meaningful challenge and get your hands dirty. When the unexpected happens and the heat and pressure are on you find out who you really are. This is your chance to grow—embrace it!

A power outage, an illness, a flight delay, a natural disaster—none of these things can be prevented entirely, but you CAN make con-tingency plans. You can rehearse and have procedures ready for things like security risks, server crashes, and accidents. That way when something does happen, instead of being completely caught off-guard and panicking, you can be calm and resourceful and bounce back quickly. Spending a little currency to prepare for the unexpected can be an investment in the future that pays off when you don't have to spend days or weeks dealing with the aftermath.

There's a fine line between staying present and being prepared for the future. On one hand, you want to focus on what you're doing so you do a good job. On the other hand, you want to think ahead and be ready for whatever comes. So how do you balance that? With nonnegotiables.

Think of the North Star. It's always there. The skies around it can change according to season, but the North Star stays the same. I have a few North Stars in my life—things that always stay the same, which I will not compromise. Like my training and my dedication to my team.

What are the North Stars in your life? Those nonnegotiable things that you live by. Maybe they revolve around your family or your business. Maybe you steadfastly attend church every week. Once you know what your nonnegotiables are, everything else is on the table. Then you know what activities you can possibly cut out of your schedule. Ask yourself the following questions when looking at the activities on your schedule:

- What is the final goal for this day? This project? This month? This year?

- Will the things I do today contribute to that goal?

- What can I do to prepare myself for my future goals?

- Am I still on track with the tasks I'm in charge of?

- Who is looking to me for answers, and how can I help them do well today and in the future?

It is hard to take the time to prepare when you stay so busy you barely have time to think. That's why I have a couple of pauses built in to my day, literal 15-minute chunks of time scheduled in my calendar where I do nothing but re-center and ask myself these questions so I stay on track.

Managing Your Time to Be On Time

It's also important to be purposeful in the way you manage and protect your own time—and the time of the team you manage. I use four simple practices to keep things running smoothly—prioritize, set boundaries, plan ahead, and train for the transitions.

PRIORITIZE YOUR TIME

As I've said before, when you say yes to something, you're saying no to something else. Find a system that works for you, whether it's setting reminders, making a checklist, or blocking your time into sections where you'll focus on certain things. You'll find that prioritizing your time doesn't tie you up like you may think. It actually frees you to focus completely on the task at hand knowing that there's time built in to your day, week, or month for the next thing.

SET BOUNDARIES

The second way you can manage your time is by setting boundaries in your personal and professional lives. Before committing to something, consider how saying yes to one thing will impact everything else in your life. This helps you clarify your expectations, then communicate them clearly to others.

PLAN AHEAD

Planning ahead is one of the biggest time-savers there is, because when you know what's coming and have allowed time for it in your schedule, it gets done. It's not as overwhelming as looking at the whole task at once. So find a scheduling or calendar system that works for you— and use it. It's like giving yourself a gift. Planning ahead gives you the space and freedom to be present where you are. You know what's ahead. You know what's coming. When you don't plan ahead, you miss things, and you don't engage with the world around you because you're too busy pushing the panic button.

Life has a cadence to it. It's like a race. When you're prepared for it, you can get in a rhythm and just go. You don't even have to think about it.

And I tell my team that I'm in it 100%. I won't tell them to do something I wouldn't do. I'm right there with them, and we're doing it together.

Train for the Transitions

Time is gained or lost in the transitions.

This concept never became clearer to me than when I started training for triathlons. Triathlons have three main sections—swimming, biking, and running. Participants must be well trained for each section of the race. It's great if you're a strong swimmer, a skilled biker, and a fast runner. But if you're not prepared, the transitions will absolutely kill you.

Ironman Triathlons start with swimming. Depending on the water temperature, that often means you're fully suited up in a wetsuit, swim cap, and goggles. When you come out of the water, you immediately sprint to your bike, shed the wetsuit, swim cap, and goggles, fasten your bike helmet onto your head, shove your feet into your shoes, snap them into the clipless pedals on your bike, grab your sunglasses, and push off.

This is a complex transition. Have you ever tried taking off a wetsuit when you're full of adrenaline, pulse pounding, and trying to move as quickly as you can? It's intense. It's awkward. It can be an absolute train wreck if you're not prepared.

If you've trained for it, you can get it done in under five minutes.

If you haven't, good luck.

Be Willing to Be a Change Agent

Life is a series of transitions, big and small. That's how I view it—one big transition from A all the way to Z. I didn't always train for the transitions. It was definitely something I learned along the way. I guess in my head I compartmentalize things, and that's how I operate in business too. If I need to turn around a company, if that's the transition, I can do it as long as I have the business outcomes and the back end in mind. I prep myself so when I go into a job, my gut starts to boil like it does before a physical race. I can feel it, and I know if I don't feel the emotion, it means I don't care. If I don't feel it, then I know I'm not taking it seriously enough.

Throughout the course of your life you'll go through several major transitions, from single to married, student to worker, kid-free to parent. We make countless transitions in a day, too, small ones like going from home to work and back again. Even though they're small in the overall scheme of things, being ready and prepared with a transition plan can save you SO much time.

On Sunday nights, I feel myself transitioning to being ready for work Monday morning. My whole body starts gearing up 24 hours ahead of time, preparing for whatever the work week will hold. I want to be ready to pivot as things get thrown at me. Just like an Ironman, I'm already thinking ahead, sometimes even three, four, five years out.

Time and Your Team

You are the leader of your team—at work, at home, at play. That means you have to set the standard and be the example. As a leader, it's possible to push too hard and pressure your team into putting in impossible hours. But you can also fall into being too lenient and allowing bad time management habits. I've seen leaders wear 80-hour work weeks like a badge of honor. They stumble around jacked up on caffeine and nicotine, humble bragging about how they pulled two all-nighters that week with their teams working 18- to 20-hour days. That does not impress me. No one can keep that up. It's not healthy. Whether you're working for a corporation, running your own business as an entrepreneur, or just managing your household and family's lives, you can't work 24/7.

I reward my team for results. At the end of the day, it's the results that matter, not how many hours you worked to get them. People tend to think they have to work all night to prove their worth. I don't like that. Results speak for themselves. If you're on my team, I don't want you up all night. I'm not rewarding you for being a hero. What's important are the results you produce and how you feel about those results. Have you put in the work to build something you can be proud of, something that will help make the world a better place? Good. That's all I ask.

On the other hand, some leaders aren't firm enough with their teams when it comes to managing their time well. I've seen this over and over again in corporations I've worked with. I inherit teams who may have been functioning within their corporations for a long time. They have set-in-stone behavior patterns. Sometimes they're good...but not always. It's my job to get those teams operating at a high level, and sometimes that means being creative with how I manage my inherited teams.

We were eight minutes into a meeting when Paul walked in late. It was my first week with this new team, and I knew I needed to set a precedent.

"Hello, Paul," I said. "Nice of you to join us."

He was mortified and turned a bright shade of pink as he stammered an apology. But I wasn't done yet.

"You have our attention now," I said with a kind smile. I was going to make an example of him, but I'm not a mean person. I wanted that moment to be memorable, not malicious. "Why don't you come up here and sing for us. Everyone who's late has to sing us a song."

Paul was late twice. He sang "Twinkle, Twinkle" in front of a boardroom full of his colleagues twice. And then he was never late again. It was my gentle way of saying, "Look, you know what you're doing. You're responsible for your time. You can do better." I've also closed the doors and locked people out two minutes after a meeting started, or required the team member to pay a dollar for every minute they were late. Just a quiet reminder that all our time is important.

I think I got that from my mother. She's an extremely classy lady. She'll never come out and say what she's really thinking, but if you've displeased her, you know it. If you show up late to her house for dinner, she'll be sweet. She'll be kind. But you'll never get invited back to her house. She's not confrontational, but she gets her point across.

The Importance of Time Around the World

The atmosphere in the boardroom was tense. The way the executive at the head of the table was watching the clock, the vein on the side of his right temple bulging every time he tightened his jaw, it wasn't likely to get better anytime soon.

I was in Shanghai with my team for a meeting with head of the Chinese division of the company I was working for. I had made sure my team was prepped, ready, and early for the meeting. We went through the customary greetings, which included meaningful handshakes complete with full eye contact and bowing of the head. The director expressed his deep honor at our presence, and we assured him that the honor was all ours. Everything seemed to be going smoothly.

There was no discernable reason for the sweat that was beading at his hairline or the nervous way his employees whispered back and forth to each other, furtively glancing up at the clock every few minutes. When we sat down at the boardroom table, the three empty seats made it obvious.

Part of his team was late.

His assistants brought in refreshments, and we talked among ourselves. Eventually, small talk petered out, and the director's agitation mounted. After several hushed phone calls where despite the language barrier it was very apparent how the director felt about the situation, he stormed out in a rage. We did not meet that day.

When you work or travel internationally, pay attention to that culture's mentality about time. In Asian countries, lateness is a serious offense. If you show up late to a meeting, they will not listen to you. They're very disciplined with their time, and I deeply respect that. Every culture has its own take on time. In Asia, time is very precious. Not only do they value punctuality, they also work long, hard hours. It's a status symbol to work a lot of hours there. They're at work until ten or eleven every night, even if they have nothing to do, because it makes them look important to their friends and families. (It's kind of scary how similar our Western culture is becoming.)

In India, on the other hand, time is always moving. It never ends, and crews work around the clock. It's like the city is on fire, and instead of rushing in to put it out, everyone's just pouring gasoline on the flames. Go, go, go!

Time never stops moving. Once it's gone, you can't get it back. I challenge you to consciously choose how you spend your time, and value other people's time as much as your own. It's a secret key to living an extraordinary life. One without a single minute wasted.

FOCUS STATEMENT
I consciously choose
to use my "time currency" wisely.

4

LISTEN FIRST

Hate to Break it To You,
But You Might Need a Hearing Aid

The woman walked into a strategy meeting in the Silicon Valley and launched right into a pitch for her new book. Too bad no one was there to buy books. (Awkward.)

My team and I were in the middle of an advertising briefing with a company we were getting ready to do business with. The room was full of top executives ready to get to work. Instead of sitting down and taking in the information being shared to see if we were the type of audience who'd be interested in her book, she launched right into her sales script. She was convinced that we'd all be spell-bound and whip out our credit cards then and there.

We watched her totally self-destruct, and all I could think was, *My god, she's not even listening.*

Everyone has a story. It's important for people to share their stories, especially if what they've learned will be valuable to others. The problem was, this woman didn't take the time to connect with or even understand who was in the room. She assumed people would want to listen to her just because of who she was. Instead, the opposite was true. Everyone was instantly turned off by it, and I still hear about it in certain circles to this day.

That situation made a huge impression on me. I still remember how annoyed and disrespected I felt. I didn't know her. I wasn't familiar with her story. She just assumed that what she had to say was more important than the meeting. In that moment, I realized one key thing:

People remember how you make them FEEL.

I vowed that I would never command someone's attention like that unless I had first put in the work to connect with and listen to them first.

Honestly, I'm never going to read that woman's book. It might be really good, but I was so annoyed that I can't look past the impression she made. Had she spent some time listening and learning about the group before responding, she'd have had a much better chance of interacting with interested listeners at the end of the meeting.

Listening can be hard. We always want to have the first—and last—word. But if you want to successfully reach your goals in any situation, train yourself to listen first, then respond.

Good listeners can be hard to find. It's kind of a lost art, and one that, in my opinion, needs to be resurrected. In my own life, I operate under the assumption that listening is THE most important first step in any conversation. I've developed a three-step process that not only makes others around me feel understood and validated, but also helps me process and react wisely.

Step 1: Get the Facts

The first step to listening has nothing to do with the information being shared and everything to do with the listener's frame of mind. People generally listen in one of two ways: to react and respond or to hear and understand. How would you rather be listened to?

Listening to react and respond is the most common form, and I see it on a daily basis. People who do this have one goal in mind—to formulate a response while the other person is speaking so they can weigh in with their two cents immediately when the speaker stops talking. This results in two people talking but not really communicating.

You can tell if someone is listening to react and respond if they don't make eye contact, start to break into the conversation to share their opinion before the speaker is done talking, or always has a better example or one-up story waiting for every lull in the conversation.

If you chronically listen to react and respond, you will find your mind wandering during the conversation, because you're busy formulating the perfect response to what they're saying. You would have a hard time repeating back what was just shared, because you were too busy thinking about how to react.

People who only listen to react and respond are not good listeners. You're unlikely to turn to them in a crisis or when you need sound advice, because you often feel like they're only listening to get what's in it for them. You don't feel heard.

On the other hand, people who listen to hear and understand make up a much smaller segment of the population. They're the ones who are sought after as good listeners. They're the ones engaged in the conversation and not on their iPhone constantly, leaning forward, making eye contact, and responding with relevant comments or questions to help them better learn and understand your thoughts. At times, they may paraphrase what you just said to ensure they're understanding you well.

People who listen to hear and understand don't have a personal agenda. They just want to be there and listen as a way of respecting the speaker and the information they're giving. They may not respond immediately when the speaker stops talking, because they're very deliberate in processing the information before they respond.

When you're in conversation with someone who listens to hear and understand, you feel valued and important. You often seek out this type of listener because you know you'll always get a thoughtful, caring response.

BOOST YOUR LISTENING STRATEGY

Not sure you're the greatest listener? The good news is, listening is a skill that can be learned and developed. There are many effective strategies to help yourself become a better listener. One strategy I use is active meditation.

Running or swimming helps put my brain into a zen state where my alpha and beta waves fade away. When my body is in a cadence and actively moving, what's going on around me takes a back seat to what's going on in my mind. I'm actively meditating. By keeping my body busy, my brain can tune in deeper to what's going on inside. Active meditation allows me to really zone out the physical and listen to myself. My running and swimming sessions are just as much about creating time to listen to myself and to plan, strategize, and problem solve as they are to train my body.

Everyone has something that helps them think and process. Sometimes it's going for a walk, taking a shower, listening to a certain kind of music. Whatever it is for you, do it. Make time and space in your life to grow your focus, because it will help you become a better listener.

Step 2: Process the Information

Once you've listened for the facts, the next step is to process what they have said. You've heard the person speak, now you have to decide what to do with the information. If you only consider the words they utter though, you'll miss other cues that can help you get a more complete, holistic view of what you're hearing. Paying attention to nonverbal cues will help you take the information you've heard and process it accurately.

VISUAL AND AUDIO CUES

These include the speaker's voice, facial expressions, and body language. These nonverbal cues can be easy to miss, but they can be absolutely pivotal in determining the meaning and nuances of your interaction. When I'm interacting with people, I'm not just listening with my ears. I'm listening with my eyes and watching people's body language. I look for eye contact and openness. In a boardroom, these visual cues can be what shows you if someone is on the up and up or if they're planning on striking at you like a cobra when your back is turned.

SETTING AND BACKGROUND INFORMATION

As you process the conversation, do a mental check of what setting and background information might come into play. What else do you know about the situation? What else do you know about the person speaking? Are there circumstances or events in their lives that may be important to consider as you seek a well-rounded assessment of the situation? It's very easy to make assumptions and misspeak if you don't know what's going on in that person's life. Consider any relevant information that may factor into your assessment.

ASK QUESTIONS TO CLARIFY

If you're not sure about something that was just said, there's nothing wrong with asking a question or two about what you've heard. It helps the speaker feel important and validated, because when you're not afraid to repeat back or ask questions, you're showing your commitment to providing a good listening ear. And sometimes a simple question can change the course of your life.

When I was in my twenties and thirties, I used to fly in to various locations for meetings, spend four straight days in a boardroom, then fly out. I'll never forget the day that another CEO asked me a simple question that altered the way I did business travel forever.

"So, Rhonda, what have you seen while you've been here? Have you been to the Taj Mahal?"

I was tempted to bristle, throw up a defense, and answer back with a scathing, "How can I go sightseeing? I'm here to do a job." But I didn't. I paused and reflected on the question. What HAD I seen in all my travels around the world?

Nothing.

I hadn't seen anything.

Oh, I'd seen conference rooms all over the world. I'd seen the inside of hotels and elevators and cabs and airports. But in all my travels, I'd never taken the time to really SEE the world. I was dumbfounded at the realization. Of course their response was disbelief.

"What? You didn't go to the Taj Mahal yet? You didn't see the Great Wall when you were in China? You've never seen the Kremlin?"

I hadn't. I'd lived in places around the world for big chunks of time, places like London and India, but I'd never really SEEN them. I was too busy working.

After that encounter, I literally cancelled the whole team's schedule for the day, loaded them in buses, and took them to the Taj Mahal.

In that moment, I pivoted and determined to make a change. Since that day, whenever I travel internationally, I have committed to cultural immersion and have set aside time for the team to really experience life in the countries we travel to. Listening attentively and then processing what had been said to me changed my life.

Step 3: React

"Rhonda, I want to show you something," said Laurie, a high-level tech executive for a company I had recently onboarded. I followed her to her office, and she sat me down in the chair across from her desk.

I really liked Laurie. We had a connection and a synergy in our working relationship right away. She has since become one of my close friends, but at the time, I had no idea what she was about to show me.

"I trust you, Rhonda. I can tell you know what you're doing. Folks in this company are hungry for leadership, real leadership, and I know you can provide that," she said earnestly. "I know what this company needs when it comes to tech. I know what will turn it around. And I also know you will listen to me."

Laurie proceeded to detail what the company called a High-Touch Model. The company we were working for dealt personally with customers. They were big on actual contact and personal attention. Laurie was proposing we restructure the company's tech to match the interpersonal structure of customer relations, but I had no idea how that would work.

How do you make something cut-and-dried like technology high touch?

I looked at Laurie's facial expression. She was completely open, with eye contact to the max. I could tell she really believed this was the best path. I thought about the background of the situation. Things were bad. They always are by the time they call me in. If we didn't do something drastic, this corporation wasn't going to make it. Thousands and thousands of people around the world would lose their jobs. There was really only one way I could respond.

"Tell me everything."

THE MOMENT OF TRUTH

There comes a point in every conversation where it's time for me to weigh in. As a full-contact leader, I owe it to my team and those I work with to give the best response I can. I cut out all the background noise, and in my mind I focus in on four main questions. Here's how this all played out in my conversation with Laurie and her team about the High-Touch Model.

QUESTION 1:
WHAT IS THE PRIORITY IN THIS SITUATION?

As I looked at Laurie sitting across from me, her eyes were pleading for me to listen. I could tell she was completely confident in her assessment of the situation and what was needed. Right now, the priority in this situation was that I listen to her.

QUESTION 2:
WHAT RESPONSE WILL HELP ACCOMPLISH THE BEST RESULTS FOR EVERYONE INVOLVED IN THIS SITUATION?

As Laurie explained the High-Touch Model and how we could potentially put it to work in our department, I could tell the idea was worth pursuing. Whenever you can integrate internal policy and preserve the culture of a company, no matter the dire straits they're in, you've won. I listened closely and responded positively as she explained her plan, then asked her if she'd be willing to work one-on-one with me to implement it.

QUESTION 3:
IS MY REACTION RESPECTFUL TO THE OTHER OTHER PERSON?

Laurie had been with the company for years. She knew the ins and outs. Although I was the CTO called in to turn things around, she had been the expert on all the goings on of the company for the past few years. I wouldn't dream of disrespecting that by pushing my way over everything else.

QUESTION 4:
HOW WILL MY RESPONSE BE PERCEIVED?

I knew my response would be well received. We both walked out of that meeting with a strong appreciation for the other person, and that was the beginning of years of successful partnerships in the industry. Together, we developed a system that designed this corporation's technology to be personal, uncomplicated, and unintimidating.

Listening in Crisis

The situation with Laurie turned out well for everyone. But not every situation can be tied up in a neat little bow. Sometimes everything hits the fan and you're thrown instantly into crisis mode. What do you do then?

Listening during a crisis requires toughness, objectivity, and grit. You have to think of it like triage in your head. Handle the most urgent matters first, and work your way down the list, listening to hear and understand, processing, and reacting as you go. It's not easy, but don't be afraid to jump in. This is what builds strength. This is what builds character. This is what sets you apart. This is grit and grind. When handled well, a crisis can be used as a tool to overcome and strengthen teams. But you have to be prepared and go in with a plan.

Like most people in America, I'll never forget where I was when the Twin Towers fell on September 11, 2001. I was in Ohio at the time in a network operation center. We were getting ready to announce a big merger of two major banks. I looked over at the big screens and there it was on TV, the towers falling. All the alarms in the network went off, then everything got disconnected.

We all knew what that meant. When the Twin Towers fell, much of the financial tech that the East Coast depended on was run from that building. With the towers collapsed and fiber-optics severed, the banks and ATMs couldn't operate. The New York Stock Exchange couldn't trade. It was time to take action.

We mobilized a team, and as soon as we could rent a car, we were on our way from Ohio to New York to get a data center back up so the financial world could continue operating.

You do what you have to do in the moment. You tackle the biggest monster first, then put out the smaller fires as you go. I went in with a biohazard suit and a mask and crawled on the ground, physically running cables from the temporary data center to the Stock Exchange building to help get things back in action. Tensions were high. Everyone was scared and on alert, but we knew it had to be done, so we did it. I was 31 years old.

BREATHE

The key strategy I use before I respond in a crisis is simply to breathe. People tell me they can see it coming—my lungs fill with air as I inhale, and after I exhale, I speak. This comes naturally to me now, but it didn't always. It was something I learned to do in the middle of a crisis, and I've practiced it ever since.

Taking that deep breath before responding has saved me from saying things I regret, speaking before thinking, and responding in a way that would hurt the situation instead of help it. It's such an easy strategy—anyone can do it from wherever they are in the world. If you need a longer pause, excuse yourself for a moment and take it.

I've learned to expect the unexpected and even welcome it. Everything important I've learned in my career has been through a crisis. Embrace it. Let the heat and the pressure shape and polish you like carbon becoming diamond. If you embrace it, it won't destroy you. It will strengthen you. So what if you get thrown off-kilter? That happens, and in my opinion it's a good thing. Operating completely out of your comfort zone means growth.

No Regrets Listening

I'm not a perfect listener by any means, but I want to live with no regrets knowing that I did what it took to really hear and understand someone. I'm also willing to admit when I haven't listened well. I'll ask questions when they need to be asked, even if they seem silly. And it's never, ever a waste to invest time in others. I'm always so grateful for the time others invest in me.

Listening in Other Cultures

Listen, process, and respond is a great way to make sure you're accurately addressing each situation. But the time you have for each step can vary depending on who you're working with. Each culture has a unique response time. In Denmark, for example, the pace is pretty slow. People value taking their time there.

What the American culture sees as normal, an Asian culture sees as slow and rude, because they run on speed and innovation. If you don't acknowledge or respond to an email within 30 minutes, they assume you don't want to work with them. The time in India and Asia runs at top speed around the clock. They never sleep, even the executives, so they expect immediate responses.

When you're moving quickly, it can be tricky to listen and process before you respond. That's when trusting your instincts and listening to your gut comes in handy. Learn to assess things quickly and respond in a timely fashion, even if it's just to say that you're out of the office and will get back to them by a certain time, then keep your word.

Study the cultural expectations on listening and response time before you travel. There are tons of resources you can refer to including books, websites, and online courses. Lumen Learning, The Center for Intercultural Dialogue, and Cultural Synergies all have great websites you can access before, or even during, travel. This will save you a lot of time and mental stress because you'll be prepared to be professional before you even step one foot off the airplane.

Listen in All Areas of Life

The concept of listening first applies in every area of life—at home, at work, and at play. Even in my Ironman Triathlon races, there's a deep element of listening so that you're prepared for the race, know the rules, and know what to do if the unexpected happens.

After you check in, you have to sit through mandatory briefing on the course. You can't proceed to the race unless you listen to the briefing. Most people are very focused and listen intently. But others are on their phones or messing around during the briefing. Big mistake. Those are the people I see later on the side of the road. They didn't listen, so they weren't prepared for the rough terrain or the altitude.

Listening is Free

When you don't listen first, everything suffers—relationships, finances, emotional health—yet listening is something everyone can do. It doesn't cost a thing besides a bit of time and attention, and the consequences of not listening are completely preventable. Don't live with regret that you didn't listen. Make listening first a part of your daily cadence. It shows people you value and respect them and it can save you from making bad decisions or embarrassing mistakes.

Don't Forget to Listen to Yourself

Life can be crazy. There are a lot of voices vying for your attention. Don't let them tune out your own. It's valuable. Listening to your gut can literally save your life.

One evening, I sat down on the beautiful antique couch, put my feet up, grabbed my red pen, and prepared to read through some of the content for this book. It was my first night at Sabora, the safari tent resort I was staying at in preparation for the 55-mile women's run the next day. It had been a really busy day, so I was ready to relax. As I flipped through the first few pages, I just couldn't get comfortable.

Rhonda, you need to get up and move to the other couch. I pushed the thought aside. There was nothing wrong with this couch. I was all settled, and getting up again would take my focus away from where I wanted it—on the manuscript. But the thought wouldn't leave.

Rhonda, go sit on the other couch.

I gave a huff. Fine. I grabbed the manuscript, my pen, and my tea and resettled myself on the couch in the center of the tent. Within a half hour, the wind suddenly picked up, and an unexpected storm rolled across the Serengeti without warning. The tent began shuddering against the rainy gusts of wind, causing the tapestries and paintings to slap against the canvas walls. Just as I heard a shout from my bodyguard outside, a flash of lightning split the sky and one of the tent poles behind the couch I had been sitting on pitched forward and fell over.

Had I not listened to my gut, it would have fallen right on top of me.

Truth is, we all have stories like this, don't we? We can all name times we did or didn't listen to ourselves and recount how our decisions affected our lives. Listening to yourself isn't something you should push aside. You're a strong, trustworthy person. You're worth listening to.

FOCUS STATEMENT
I listen first before responding.

5

BE HONEST
You CAN Handle the Truth

"I feel like a hobbit down here," my team member Gerry grumbled as he ducked—again—to avoid hitting his hard hat on the ceiling of the tunnel. I laughed.

"See?" I said. "There are advantages to being short. Besides, this was your bucket list item, remember?"

My team and I were in South Korea holding meetings with affiliates for the company we were working for at the time, and it was our day off. We decided to dress in traditional Korean clothing and headed out to visit a small village near the border between South Korea and North Korea. As we approached the border, miles and miles of razor wire came into view, stretching into the distance as far as the eye could see. On the other side of the wire was a two-and-a-half-mile expanse of no-man's land that stretched the entire length—160 miles of the two countries' shared border. We had reached the DMZ.

As much as I had teased Gerry about his desire to visit the land-marks of one of the most historically hostile locations in the world, I was fascinated too. There was no way we were going to miss out on the chance to visit the area. You could take guided tours from the village we were going to, and Moon Son, one of our colleagues who is ex-military, got us in on one at the last minute.

The DMZ (demilitarized zone) is one of the most eerie places I've ever been. The borders on either side bristle with armed soldiers, artillery and weapons all aimed at the other country, just in case. The level of unease is palpable, and for good reason. There is no trust here. At that time, landmines lay hidden in the expanse between countries, propaganda was blasted at each side through giant speakers, and balloon campaigns were known to drift over the zone, raining writ-ten political literature on the other side.

Over 60 years of lies and dishonesty all line up and point at each other day in and day out, rain or shine, but nothing illustrates the level of subterfuge and mistrust here more clearly than the tunnels. Since 1974, four underground tunnels have been discovered deep underground originating from North Korea. Experts believe they were designed to help move massive numbers of troops—up to 30,000 an hour—into South Korea. Each tunnel has been walled off, but you can take guided tours of three of them.

So of course, down into a tunnel Gerry, our teammate Charles, and I went. It's an intense experience. You feel like you're descending at a 90-degree angle, to about 150 feet below the surface. The tunnels are about seven feet by seven feet, but Gerry is over six feet tall, and with a hard hat on, it was a tight fit. We climbed down all the way to where the tunnel was walled off by the South Koreans, and when we turned around, I heard Gerry groan behind me as he realized we now had to climb back up. Gerry and I have done some runs together, so we decided to make a race of it. We were both sweating and short of breath when we burst out of the tunnel into the freezing winter air.

As soon as we emerged to the surface, our phones' notifications started sounding. I wiped my forehead one last time and pulled my jacket tighter as I dug in my pocket for my phone. A message from my mom flashed across the screen, and when I read it, my blood ran colder than the air.

"Rhonda, are you okay? Where are you? Check in with me, okay? I just saw on the news that North Korea launched a nuclear test across the DMZ at South Korea."

It was February 2016, and tensions were high. The threat of nuclear missile launches seemed to simmer just under the surface, and we had unknowingly been underground in the DMZ during the first nuclear test missile launch. Needless to say, we breathed a sigh of relief as we left the area.

As we drove away, I couldn't help but feel a deep sense of sadness. Decades of mistrust had eroded the relationship between the two countries to the point that there was no honesty between them. On the surface, everything looked pretty calm. Everyone was on their own sides. Agreements were signed. Barricades were respected. Meanwhile, deep underground lie four tunnels that serve as a testament that nothing is as it seems. Trust nothing.

The Truth About Lies

Dishonesty breeds uncertainty and mistrust. Nothing good can survive in that kind of an atmosphere—not in your business or your personal life. Lies are damaging. Instead of seeking healing and wholeness, a lie attempts to cover up something that could otherwise have been fixed or repaired. Lies don't allow for transformation. They keep you locked up, imprisoned by a false reality that doesn't allow for growth and development.

There's no room for lies in full-contact living. The grit and grind will chew you up and spit you out if you don't have an honest foundation to rely on.

Honesty is the gold standard in life, in work, and in any situation you might face anywhere in the world. Of course, we all strive to be honest. We all want to be living, speaking examples of integrity and truth to people around us. But that's really difficult sometimes. And if we're willing to admit it, the first and worst lies we tell are the ones we tell ourselves.

"What do you mean, Rhonda? I don't lie to myself. How is that even possible?"

Sure you do. We all do. And we're so good at it. At some point or another, we've all convinced ourselves of something that's not true... and it needs to stop.

Lies We Tell Ourselves

It's a familiar story. She has a good job. She enjoys it...kind of. Okay, so it's not really lighting her up, but it pays the bills. She tells herself she should be grateful for this job. The pay is good, and besides, if she leaves it, she won't be able to find anything better. Every day she wakes up, drinks a cup of coffee, and drives to work, counting the hours until she can come home again. She tells herself that's just the way it is for everyone, but she secretly envies her friends who love talking about their jobs and the fulfillment they find in their work. Sometimes she wonders what it would be like if she walked away from her dead-end job. She'd go back to school and get her teaching degree—she's always loved helping kids learn. Then she hears her dad's voice in her head, "Teaching doesn't pay the bills. Better get a good job."

Lies tend to follow us from the past into our futures, year after year, until eventually we accept them as truth and they define us. We convince ourselves the lies start with us, that they're just part of who we are. But many times they're lies that were pushed on us from someone else, either purposefully or unintentionally. And instead of acknowledging the lies and calling them out for the falsehoods they are, we just feed ourselves a steady diet of the same.

- I'm not good enough.

- I don't have it in me to go all-in. I just don't think I could do it.

- I'll never achieve more than this level of performance, so why even try?

- I don't need to take care of my health right now. I'll do it when I get older.

- If I try and fail, I'll never have another chance to get it right.

- I need to try to keep everyone else happy, otherwise things will fall apart.

- I only need to do the bare minimum. It won't make a difference if I don't give 100%.

Any of those sound familiar?

It's time to get honest with yourself. Good or bad, the truth matters. If you've been selling yourself short and stunting your own growth, you need to shut that down right now and step up to the plate in your own life. If you've been inflating yourself and turning a blind eye to things that need work, acknowledging the truth is the first step toward humbly dealing with your faults and becoming the person you're meant to be.

Spotting the Real vs. the Fake

We live in a strange time. "What you see is what you get" has given way to "what you see is what I want you to see."

Yes, I'm talking about social media. Picture-perfect snapshot selfies, polished prose posts, and overinflated profile descriptions are so easy to create—too easy. We log in and log out, leaving a trail of accomplishments and achievements out for the world to see and conveniently omitting the gritty mess of daily struggle.

It leaves us with nothing but a hollow sense of reality. Who can live up to that? It's not real. Oh, maybe it's a prettier or more sanitized view of our life, but when we leave out the challenges and failures, we leave out our humanity. We leave out the very things that cause us to grow and learn and get stronger.

Don't get me wrong, I enjoy a good selfie as much as anyone. People who travel with me are always teasing me when I pull the car over to snap a shot of an interesting landmark or beautiful vista. And it's true—I created a traffic jam in India just for a photo.

Those become fun memories and keepsakes that I treasure because they were real experiences I had with people I care out.

It's important to capture those things, but don't be afraid to be genuinely you. What the world really needs is the true, authentic YOU.

Sniffing Out the Truth

Honesty is right, but that does not mean it's easy. Sometimes it means having to deliver bad news. Sometimes it means facing things you don't want to. Sometimes it means cleaning up big messes. Sometimes it even means letting someone go. Be honest anyway. The people in your life and on your team are worth it.

What does being honest look like in terms of a grit-and-grind lifestyle? It looks like facing things even when you don't feel like it. Like doing the hard thing even when it requires sacrifice. Like making accurate assessments and then taking positive action.

It's really so basic—just tell the truth.

Be honest with yourself and everyone around you.

It might be the hardest thing you've ever done, but the truth will set you free.

FOCUS STATEMENT
I value truth and
commit to full transparency.

6

BE
ACCOUNTABLE
Get Ready For the Straight Uphill Climb

CHAPTER 6

Sometimes life feels like the bike portion of the St. George Ironman Triathlon. It starts out all rolling hills and scenic vistas, then dips down through St. George and flattens out to a fast stretch where you muscles sing and you can't wipe the grin off your face because everything is so beautiful and crisp and pure.

Then you hit the incline. What had been smooth sailing now takes a sharp uphill ascent through Snow Canyon State Park, and while the scenery is great, discounting the difficulty of this hill would be a big mistake. This section of the race is the real deal, and if you're not ready for it, it could quite literally be the death of you.

When you race, you're riding a piece of equipment that's precisely calibrated for the road—thin tires, curled handlebars, finely tuned shifters. And clipless pedals. If you've never experienced clipless pedals, they're a major lifesaver on the straightaways. They are made to go with special shoes that clip straight into the pedal, keeping your feet from slipping off and allowing the force of your muscles to not only push down on the top of the rotation but also to pull from the bottom.

I had heard about this section of the course. I had trained for it. But nothing really prepares you for what it's actually like. Imagine pedaling, clipped in, up an incline so steep that it seems like you're pedaling straight up the side of a mountain. Your legs ache. Your lungs burn. And then the other racers around you start dropping off.

I saw racer after racer give up, unclip their pedals, hop off their bikes, and walk the rest of the way up. Those were the ones who voluntarily got off their bikes. I watched many, many others, professionals even, crash and burn, literally falling off the side of the course. When you go down, it happens so fast, you don't have time to unclip your shoes and catch yourself. It gets ugly.

I found out later that six people broke their collar bones on that race. I had challenged six of the men on my team to do it with me, and two of them backed out before the race even started—and they live in Utah! But who could really blame them?

I watched all of this happening around me, and my mind started protesting. *This is ridiculous, Rhonda. You're going to kill yourself! Just hop off and walk. No one expects you to tough this out. It's too much.* I had a choice to make. Would I give up, perhaps avoiding a nasty fall, and walk the rest of the way up the mountain? Or would I stay accountable to the goal I had set and grit and grind it out?

I battled with myself for an intense two minutes, but when the dust cleared, I was still on that bike, and I was not going to allow myself to get off. I shut everything out, and I refused to feel the pain and fear for the next four miles upward. That was the hardest thing I've ever done in my life, because as hard as I had trained, as well prepared as I thought was, the battle was won right there in the midst of the race inside my mind. Mental toughness at its finest.

The only person I was accountable to was myself, but if I couldn't keep my commitments to myself, how would I do so with others? I rode all 56 miles of that course—and so did the other four members of my team. And when we reached the summit, everyone was screaming. All I could think was, *I did it! Oh my god, I can conquer anything!*

I still use that experience today to motivate me. When I'm tempted to throw in the towel or take the easy way out, I remember that absolutely excruciating stretch of the St. George Ironman and how none of the pain and strain and fear mattered when I reached the finish line.

What Does Being Accountable Look Like?

Comments like, "They need to be held accountable for their actions" or "I need an accountability buddy" frustrate me. Accountability isn't something that's applied to you. It's not something that someone else holds you to or a concept that keeps you in line. Accountability is something inside you. It's a way of life that encompasses responsibility, communication, and cooperation. Being accountable means you live with integrity and keep your word. You accept what comes and deal with it in an honorable way that not only respects those around you but also respects yourself.

Being accountable to yourself isn't easy. It's hard to stare pain and fear and uncertainty and blame in the face. Being accountable means you'll take the hit when necessary to protect your team. It also means you'll own up to things instead of leaving someone else with the consequences of your actions. Being accountable builds toughness and grit because it takes a willingness to put others first, admit when you're wrong, and communicate and cooperate with your team every single day.

Because being accountable takes a level of mental toughness, when I need to dig deep to honor a commitment made to myself or others, I think about how it felt when I went straight up that hill to the summit. I vividly recall how that moment felt, and I pull that emotion out and relive it so I can apply it to new situations.

I know I can succeed at whatever I'm grinding through at the moment, because I've done it before.

So what about you? When did you follow through on a promise to yourself? A time when you were really proud that you stuck it out and reached your goals? And how did it feel? What emotions come up when you remember it? Let that feeling sink in deep so you know it in your bones. And whenever you're tempted to quit or go back on a commitment, remember. Remember how good it felt when you stayed accountable. You were strong then, and you can be strong again.

Know Your Nonnegotiables

Remember when we talked about your North Star? The nonnegotiables? The things you won't compromise on, no matter what? It's critical to identify those things, because the first person you're accountable to in life is yourself. You are the first—and last—person you have to answer to every day, and you must hold true to the nonnegotiables in your life. But how can you if you've never identified what they are?

There are three main things in my life that I consider part of my "moral compass" and help me lead by example. The first is my friends and family. Second, the 10 principles in this book. Third, my physical fitness and triathlon training. Those things are my benchmarks and the things I will not compromise on. Staying accountable to how well I'm doing in these areas keeps me on track. When I get off track, I feel it.

Take my race training, for example. I run these races to keep myself sane. Training is an absolutely necessary component. If I didn't train to prepare for them, then I'd be one of the ones in the hospital instead of standing at the summit. I have to stay accountable to my training schedule, and in that way I'm staying accountable to and honoring myself, my health, and my fitness.

I've always been a fitness fanatic, but training for triathlons takes things to a new level and requires dedication, commitment, and the willingness to constantly show up, to train day in and day out. I've gotten off 15-hour flights and gone straight to the gym to get a workout in. It seems crazy to other people, but to me it's just a matter of staying accountable to myself (and kicking the jet lag).

Set Goals, Take Action, and DO

At the end of the day, YOU are the one who has to take the initiative to set goals, take action, and do what you say you're going to do. There's no app or program that can do that for you, no matter how advanced technology gets. You're the one who gets up when the alarm goes off, laces up your shoes, and heads out the door. Every day, it's up to you. Success builds on success. So if you're finding it difficult to stay true to your word—either to yourself or others—then maybe you need to start with smaller steps.

It's better to set a small, easily achievable goal and succeed than to make staying accountable a momentous task. If you tell yourself you're going to work out every day for an hour, rain or shine, that might be too much at the beginning. The first time you let it slide makes it easier for you to let it happen again. Discipline is a muscle. You have to develop it over time. Maybe you say you're going to work out four hours this week. Then you have a few options for when things get hectic. You can do one hour for four days, or you can break it up into smaller chunks over the week. Either way, you've still succeeded in staying accountable. And since it was only a one-week goal, you can adjust it the following week. The more often you do exactly what you say you're going to do, the easier it gets.

Be Accountable to Your Team

True full-contact leadership means recognizing that the buck stops with you. As the head of your team, it's your job to make sure your team meets the benchmarks and goals for the project. There are certain things I hold myself specifically responsible for. I will make sure I'm fully prepped, on time, and attentive. I will do what I said I was going to do, and I expect that same dedication out of other people on my team too. That said, when something goes wrong, I will not hesitate to step up and take the hit.

Being accountable alone is a heavy burden to bear, though. I manage very large global teams, so practically speaking, there's no way I can be responsible for everything. I have to build in a good structure in my teams so I know things are being taken care of, with every task and issue getting the attention it needs. That is not going to happen if I don't ever allow my team to take responsibility and hold themselves accountable.

I give my team members real opportunities to grow in terms of accountability by building an extra 8% margin into the innovation budget for every contract I work on. This is so important. I want to empower my teams to think for themselves, to take action, and to be responsible for the results. That fund gives my team members the confidence and willingness to step forward and try new things for the good of the project. They know I believe in them enough to back them up.

Things go wrong sometimes. I've taken hits for the team during outages, through production issues, and even for human errors that have resulted in the network crashing and putting eight teams in the field at risk. As a leader, that's just part of the job. I'm very open and honest, and I'll tell the team if I don't think something they want to try will work, but I will still back their efforts and encourage them to try. That's how you learn accountability. That's how you grow leadership. One step at a time.

You must also be accountable to your industry peers. They're the ones who know exactly what it's like to walk in your shoes. I have a circle of industry peers I rely on. They know they can call on me, and I know I can call on them. All of my deepest work bonds have been made working grit and grind through crises, and those connections are invaluable.

ENABLE HAPPINESS IN OTHERS

You have a choice in HOW you want to be accountable to your team. You can do it grudgingly and make sure your team—and everyone else—knows what a sacrifice and hardship this is for you. Or you can practice servant leadership by graciously accepting the role and care for the people you're responsible for. Whenever you can, use the accountability you show to your team to enable happiness, build unity, and facilitate team growth.

I've accepted difficult jobs before. In fact, all the jobs I take are extremely challenging. The temptation is to pass the stress and strain off to the whole team, but that's not full-contact leadership. I love the mess. I love it. I've learned to dive in hand-in-hand with my team and handle it. Usually when I get a call on a new project, it goes something like this.

"Rhonda, we have something for you. The situation is really grim. This corporation needs an overhaul in ninety days. I know that's tight, and everything is a real mess. You're going to have to come in with your team and pretty much go dark to get it done in that amount of time. Will you do it?"

I smile and check my battle scars in the mirror. Another chance to grit and grind. Yes, we can do it. I pick up the phone, and I call in my team. They never disappoint me, because they're ready. They already know it will be a mess, but they also know what we're capable of together, that I've got their backs, and that the reward on the other side of the mess is going to be so much greater than whatever cushy situation we're in at the moment.

Every time we take on a project, there's that rush of adrenaline. The race is on, and we know it's going to be a marathon, not a sprint. There will be a lot of obstacles along the way, but those challenges bring chances for growth and accomplishment—chances my team members wouldn't get otherwise. That development brings such fulfillment and satisfaction on the other side, and I love enabling that in others. And we always, always know the finish line is up ahead.

BE WILLING TO TAKE A HIT FOR THE TEAM

I will back my team no matter what, and I will make the hard choices in order to protect them. Years ago, five of my team members and I were brought in on a project with a well-known company, only to find out that the leadership there was in chaos. They refused to follow any sort of advice we had or plan we tried to set up. In fact, they resisted anything we tried to do to help them from the get-go.

The main issue was that the leadership was broadcasting successes that did not exist, and they refused to get real about their situation and deal with the issues they were facing. I wasn't going to just let that slide. I can't do my job like that. I'm not going to operate under inflated, unproven numbers. And I wasn't afraid to call them out on it. It was one of the most difficult professional situations I've ever been in.

I watched my team practically beat their heads against the wall trying to get through to the leadership of that corporation. I felt it too, and we turned ourselves inside out to try to make something work. But there are certain nonnegotiables I have with the projects I take on, and one of them is truth, and I refused to back down on that. I realized we were not going to be able to help this company and get them the results they wanted. They simply wouldn't invest. So for the sake of my team and to protect the integrity of our work, we developed an exit strategy and moved on to another company.

That was hard. I don't like to leave things like that. I take those messes as personal challenges, and I love turning things around for corporations. But it was hurting my team. They were suffering—some of my people were actually hospitalized for stress. Not long after we left, two of the main leaders we had dealt with, the company president and his right-hand man, were fired and were walked out of their own building. It was all over the news.

I'll never regret putting my team's needs ahead of my own pride and desire to get results. That's one of the reasons my teams are so solid. I have people who have followed me from company to company because they trust my leadership, they know I've got their backs, and they're willing to stand with me and be accountable for our results together.

FAIL HARD & FAIL FAST

Spoiler alert: no one is going to succeed at everything 100% of the time. At some point, you will fail, and part of being accountable is owning it, processing it, then pivoting...fast. It's okay to fail hard and fail fast because that means you're learning, growing, and trying. Good will come out of it. Lessons will be learned. It's always better to dive in and try. Then if you fail, try something else.

My team once came to me with a plan to test a new product strategy involving these Google technology glasses. I want my team to implement and try new things, so I always allow a certain percentage of the innovation budget to test and try different ideas like this. They decided to rapid-fire test the glasses at locations in Korea, but unfortunately it was a total flop. We quickly acknowledged the failure and moved on to the next thing. I was completely okay with giving them the freedom to test it out. I had my doubts about the glasses, but my team had the freedom to try, and they had the freedom to fail. They knew I would back them no matter what. That's how you learn.

Be Accountable to the Culture Around You

We're all part of a bigger world. The culture you live in has directly impacted other cultures, sometimes in good ways and sometimes in bad. You can't close your eyes to what's going on around the world. Part of being accountable for me is stepping into whatever culture I'm in—full cultural immersion—and being open and willing to be changed by it.

Several years ago, my team and I were overhauling a call center in Krakow, Poland. As I've mentioned, when we're overseas, we also take time to go out and experience the culture we're in. In this case, we wanted to understand the history behind World War II and how it has affected the way the people there live and do business today. So the first opportunity we had, we visited the Auschwitz concentration camp.

Auschwitz is the largest in a network of six concentration camps that Nazi Germany built to carry out their plan to eradicate the world of Jewish people and other groups they deemed undesirable. It's estimated that 1.5 million Jews were killed there over the course of three years.

It was one of the most humbling experiences of my life. When you visit Auschwitz, they don't hold back. The whole camp has been preserved as it really was. You see the gas chambers and the cells the prisoners were kept in, and large displays show the callous way the camp guards dealt with the prisoners' possessions and belongings.

As my friends and teammates, Gerry, Charles, Andrea, Shawn, Neeti, Mike, and I toured the Auschwitz museum, we saw a display my mind couldn't make sense of. It looked like a tangled up bunch of wires all mashed together in a big rectangle about 15 feet long and 10 feet high. As we stared at it, Gerry suddenly said, "Rhonda, you know what we're looking at? It's eyeglasses!" He was right—it was this giant mass of thousands of reading glasses that had been discarded before the Germans sent victims to the gas chambers. I was shattered at the disregard for human life that represented.

As we filed through to a display in another of the crematoriums, we were hit with one of the most horrific sights I have ever seen. Behind the glass was a giant seven-ton bale of human hair. At that point, I couldn't keep it together. How? How could a group of human beings do this to other human beings? My heart broke for everyone who'd been affected by this horrific time in human history. I knew that living in Krakow under the shadow of Auschwitz had to weigh heavily on the people there.

As we stared at that enormous bale of hair, one statement caught my attention. Seven tons of hair represents so, so many people, but we learned there had originally been even more. The tour guides told us that clothing giant Hugo Boss had actually used tons more to make uniforms for the prisoners.

I can't change what happened from 1942–1945 at Auschwitz. I wish I could. But one thing I can do is never support or buy from a company that willingly benefitted from the loss of humanity like that. I can be accountable for that much.

How to Start Being Accountable

Start right where you are. If you're a waitress, then be the best, most integrity-filled waitress you can be. Do what you're doing now to the best of your ability, and if you're not happy where you're at, keep your eyes open for that next opportunity and be ready to pivot when it presents itself. Don't be afraid of entry-level work. We all start somewhere, and earning your stripes is better preparation for leadership than any other training or experience you can get.

I wasn't born with a silver spoon in my mouth. I had a wonderful, supportive family who knew how important accountability and responsibility were. I had to work my way through college. I paid for my own car, my gas, my insurance. You know what? I thank God for that. I thank God my mother saw the wisdom in hard work and earning your way up. It helped shape me into the leader I am today.

When you earn what you have, you really own it. You can take pride in your accomplishments, and you're more aware of what it took to make it grow and what you'll need to invest in order to keep stretching and taking chances. That foundation of hard work and accountability gives you confidence when you are faced with a choice of diving into a situation that may be over your head. Knowing you earned the accomplishments you have now shows you what you're capable of and gives you courage to go even bigger next time.

Own your accountability. Learn from your mistakes. Don't be afraid to try. When you model accountability in your life, it sets a standard for your team and the people around you that shows you will do what's necessary and take care of what you're responsible for, even when it means you jump feet first into a mess and learn your way out. Even when it means owning up to your failures. Even when it means doing all the hard things. It's worth it.

Who You Surround Yourself With Matters

As the driver pulled up to the Sabora tented camp in Tanzania, I couldn't stop the smile from breaking across my face. I was back! I'd been looking forward to my return trip to the Singita Grumeti Reserve for weeks. The Serengeti Girls Run didn't start until the next day, but I'd come a day early because I couldn't wait to see the people I'd connected with on my previous trip. Helen, Khalid, Edward, Dennis, Johann, Grace. As I stepped out of the vehicle, I was greeted by smiling faces and hugs. It felt like home.

And they were ready for me. I wasn't there for very long before they asked me to go for a run with them. I hadn't been planning on running that day—I was going to be running 18 miles a day for the next 3 days in a row. It probably wasn't a great idea.

"Oh, I don't know, you guys..."

"Oh yes, let's go!" Helen, my bodyguard, beamed with a smile. "We have been training so we could run with you when you returned!"

I couldn't say no to Helen. She had stuck by my side on my previous trip, and she was one of the only conditions I had put on my return. I would be running the Serengeti Girls Run, but really, I was there for the people. I was there for Helen, and for the group of 400 school children I'd be speaking to the next day. So I laced up, and off we went for a five-mile run.

My South African friends, unbeknownst to me, had decided to run with me when I returned, so they had prepared accordingly. They'd been training since I'd returned home after the last trip. They worked together, encouraged each other, and willingly became accountable—as a team—to their goal. Now that's an example of team accountability if I've ever seen one. I was so touched.

Surround yourself with people who are willing to do the hard things and be accountable with you. The culture of those you hang around rubs off. Make sure these people will impact you positively, and that will make the easy things more fun and the hard things seem easier.

Why is Being Accountable Important?

At the most basic level, accountability matters because doing what you say you'll do and showing up responsibly day in and day out earns respect and trust. It doesn't matter if you're working with an international corporation or communicating with your spouse or kids, accountability is what shows people you're willing to dive in and do what needs to be done. It makes you someone people are willing to stand with, and that's priceless.

- Consistently do what you say you're going to do.
- Do what needs to be done, even when it's hard.
- Say what you mean and mean what you say and do.

There's no excuse for not living with accountability every day. It doesn't cost any money, doesn't require a special location or certification, doesn't need to wait for a certain time on a schedule. Understand that nothing is handed to you. You're going to have to get up and go after it. You're not accountable for everything, but you are responsible for your own actions.

What you gain with accountability is so much more than what you give. Yes, it takes hard work and humility, but in return you learn responsibility, appreciation, creativity, innovation, and intuition. You also gain the trust and respect of those around you. So get out there and earn it!

FOCUS STATEMENT

*I will stay accountable and
own my choices in every situation.*

7

COMMUNICATE OPENLY

Speak Now or Forever Hold Your Peace

Miscommunications. We've all experienced them. Sometimes they make for a really good laugh, like the time my friend's mother thought the abbreviation "LOL" meant "lots of love" and used it to sign a sympathy card for a relative who had just had surgery (It actually stands for "laughing out loud."). Other times, a miscommunication can result in the loss of revenue or reputation, as when Kentucky Fried Chicken opened their first franchises in China. No one checked the translation to their famous slogan "Finger Lickin' Good," and the Chinese translation read "Eat your fingers off." You can guess how well that went over.

In business, one of the main responsibilities that leaders have is to communicate well, and I embrace this wholeheartedly. Transparency is key. Getting the right message across at the right time in the right tone can mean millions in added revenue for a corporation, and the opposite is true as well. In your personal life, how you communicate really affects the quality of your relationships. And when high-stress situations come, like the ones I work in every day, open communication is essential.

There are so many subtle nuances that affect communication, but tackling the basics is something anyone can, and should, do. The average person needs to hear something seven to eight times to process and remember it. When you learn to communicate well, it's easy for people to trust, respect, and follow you.

So if communication is so important, why is it so hard? With all the technology available today, from video conferencing to messaging apps and team communication platforms, why does it seem like it's easier than ever to send the wrong message? You'd think that by now we humans would have this thing down, right? Despite the abundance of tech at our fingertips, it's still up to us as individuals to make sure we're communicating effectively. I like to look directly at a person's face and communicate eye to eye. Nothing can replace the responsiveness and compassion of another living soul.

I believe generational differences also contribute to the communication difficulties among family members, friends, professional teams, and people in different cultures. Studies show that each generation tends to prefer different communication platforms. Traditionalists like face-to-face interaction. Baby Boomers prefer to handle things over the phone. Generation X would rather send an email. And Millennials love social media and messaging apps. All of this means communication has to be purposeful and direct in order to reach everyone it's intended to. I always say a message sent in an email or text is never a message received.

I prefer face-to-face or voice-to-voice because there's less opportunity for miscommunication. And if someone doesn't understand me, I can quickly sort it out right then before serious problems crop up. There's no right or wrong method of communicating. The problems set in when one person doesn't understand exactly what the other is saying. Oh sure, you might understand the words, but may not comprehend the true meaning. The solution is to seek common ground.

- **BE FLEXIBLE.** Ask what type of communication the people around you prefer. Do they prefer phone or email? Text or voice app? Let them know that you want to find a platform that will work for both of you, and encourage them to be willing to meet somewhere in the middle. They'll feel heard while getting the message that they may need to adjust their communication as well.

- **TRY DIFFERENT THINGS.** Are there ways you can harness technology to deliver communication in different ways for different team members? Apps like Zapier can take messages from one platform and deliver them on another—like taking messages from a platform such as Facebook Messenger or Skype and delivering them as a text or an email.

- **PROVIDE TRAINING WHEN NEEDED.** Once everyone decides on a common platform, make sure they all know how to use it. You don't want to miss a meeting because you didn't have notifications turned on or realize that the research you needed has been stored in the cloud. A quick demonstration for your team can work wonders.

Many times we think of communication as just the output of the message we want to deliver, but that's leaving out half the equation! Listening is so important that it gets its very own chapter in this book, but it bears mentioning here as well. Often our communication is blocked because we deliver the message but forget to wait for the response, missing out on a valuable exchange that can help create the kind of open communication we really need. Don't forget to listen.

Keep an Open Mind

Even if you're a confident person—even if it's really hard to knock you down and you've lived and experienced enough to have an innate sense for what's going to work and what isn't—that doesn't mean you've seen it ALL. You must keep an open mind when you're communicating. If you go into a situation with your mind already made up and closed to other options and solutions, you've already shut down effective communication.

Be willing to be proven wrong. It's okay to say, "I don't know." There's no shame in that when you're honestly, openly communicating. People will respect you for it. Own your stuff, and when you're wrong, admit it with humility. That kind of communication breaks down the barriers between us. And then we can work together toward common goals. And isn't that what we're all really after?

Read Verbal and Nonverbal Cues

My colleague Gerry and I walked out of a conference room after a meeting for a new project. I was feeling very unsettled, but Gerry seemed unaffected. As he held the door for me on the way out, he cheerfully stated, "I think that went well. Don't you?"

I leveled my gaze at him as I passed through the double doors. "No."

His steps faltered for just a moment. "Really? Why?"

"The team leader was too busy texting to pay attention to anything going on in the meeting," I listed off my observations on my fingers as we walked. "So was the administrative assistant sitting next to him trying to read over his shoulder. The VP pretty much lied through his teeth the whole meeting. I could tell by the way he wouldn't make eye contact or shake my hand when I walked in. He's hiding something. We need to keep an eye on him."

Gerry raised his eyebrows and let out a disbelieving chuckle. "Remind me to never play poker with you." But you know what? As it turned out, that executive was lying, and he was called out on the carpet for it later.

HOW you say something is just as important as WHAT you say, and I don't just mean with words. Not all communication is verbal. When you were a kid, your mother could probably communicate a multitude of things with just a look. She could level you with a glance if you were in trouble, and she could beam confidence at you from across the room if you were nervous or scared. That's how strong nonverbal cues can be.

I've had people stand in front of me and say exactly what they knew I wanted to hear, and deep down I knew they were lying. How? Because I've learned to read nonverbal cues. I've learned to trust my gut, and I'm almost never wrong. If you're not sure you can trust what someone is telling you, look for telltale signs like fidgeting and avoiding eye contact. Those visual cues can provide subtle clues to the person's intentions.

When I walk into a room, the first thing I do is read the people in it. I watch their body language and "listen" with my eyes, looking for good eye contact and a relaxed posture. Certain other postures are an immediate tip-off that trouble is coming. Someone who sits with their arms crossed in front of their chest is going to be closed to whatever is proposed. A person who leans back with their hands crossed behind their head reminds me of a cobra—they're going to attack in the boardroom. I can read which people are plugged in to the situation and which aren't, and I know if someone says one thing but means another.

Other nonverbal cues can indicate something different altogether. We had a team member in Belgium who never spoke in meetings. It would have been easy to mistake this for being standoffish, but it was really more of a self-confidence issue. If there's someone like that on your team, make the extra effort to connect with them in a way they feel comfortable. Perhaps a phone conversation or email would be a better way to break the ice. These people may have incredibly valuable insights, but you have to communicate with them privately so they feel safe to voice their ideas. I sat down and had a heart-to-heart with this team member, and it has made all the difference.

Nonverbals can clue you in when something's off too. Once when I inherited a team, one of the members of security wouldn't speak or make eye contact. I later learned he felt unsupported and that was his way of showing it. Today, he's a superstar. He speaks his mind, and I'm so proud of him.

Visual and verbal cues are even more essential to monitor in crisis and negotiation situations. Knowing what your teammates are thinking just by a look or a glance can really come in handy during tense contract negotiations in a foreign country. Sometimes all you have the chance to do is exchange looks. Taking time in the normal day-to-day to really get to know and understand your team members' cues can be a real lifesaver in a crisis situation.

CHECK YOUR CUES

Not sure how to read someone? Or, worse yet, not sure how you're coming across to your team members and others around you? The following verbal and nonverbal cues are hallmarks of a confident, upright person and should be studied and replicated in your life. If you notice someone displaying the opposite of these, you may need to be on guard and dig deeper to find their true intentions.

VERBAL CUES	NONVERBAL CUES
Use a positive tone	Make eye contact
Match the volume to the situation	Give a firm handshake
	Dress for the occasion
Enunciate clearly	Have good posture and presence
Ask for clarification	
Speak calmly	Use appropriate facial expressions
Show interest in others	
Use humor when appropriate	Initiate interactions with others
Affirm what has been said	Give your full attention
Request feedback	Respond to others' nonverbal cues
Be present	

Clearly State Your Expectations

So many miscommunication problems happen when expectations are not clearly communicated. It puts so much pressure on someone when they're trying their hardest to perform but have no idea what the benchmarks and goals are for a task. I cannot overemphasize this—you can't manage what you can't measure.

I do my best to make sure that unspoken expectations do not exist in any of my interactions. Yes, that means the communication takes a little more time, but it definitely helps when everyone is on the same page at the beginning. And it's a huge time-saver—and sanity saver—on the back end. When everyone clearly understands the tasks and expectations set before them, I'm answering fewer questions and cleaning up fewer messes in the long run.

- **PLAN AHEAD.** The first thing I do when starting a new team assignment is slate out how long the project will take and when it should be completed. I factor in a little extra time for the unexpected, because trust me, it almost always happens.

- **BRING IN THE TEAM.** I jokingly refer to my crew as my SEAL Team because they're so highly trained in their roles. They're like Navy SEALs, and I can always count on them in a crisis. Once they're in place, I then call in the main players for the assignment—the team leaders and subcontractors who will manage the larger sections of the project. We sit down together and work backward through it. We set benchmarks along the way so there are written, attainable goals in place that can be used as targets for the progress of the project. Before we leave the meeting, I make sure the team leaders and subcontractors understand exactly what they need to communicate to those working on the smaller tasks.

- **MEET REGULARLY.** This is really important. I know the word "meeting" can seem like a dirty word, but even a short stand-up session every morning for 30 minutes can go a long way toward averting pitfalls and disasters that could slow down or even sideline a project. Stay on top of things, and make sure you're getting regular reports from the team leaders and subcontractors.

- **GIVE ADVANCE NOTICE.** If the scope of the project changes or deadlines need to shift, let the teams know right away. When team members aren't in the loop about what's going on, they tend to feel disconnected and lose their desire to give their best work. It's not fair to keep your team in the dark, and keeping on top of project changes helps avoid scope creep.

Take Ownership

Communicating expectations is part of your job as a leader, whether you're a corporate manager or basketball coach. You can't blame a team member for not performing up to standards if they never knew what the standards were. Take pride in making sure your team is the most well-informed, unified working group out there.

There will also be times when you will have to face your team and admit you were wrong or deliver news that no one wants to hear. But you must do it. Even if the situation is bad or personally embarrassing. It's part of open communication. If you mess up, admit it immediately. If people know they can trust you, they will give you grace to make mistakes. If you're not transparent with your team, they won't feel free to be transparent with you. Set the tone for how communication is going to go, and your team will follow suit.

There will also come a time when you have to deliver negative feedback to someone. It's not fun. Nobody likes to do it. But I promise you that your constructive feedback is one of the best gifts you can give to team members, and if they trust you and know your words are coming from a caring, honest place, they'll receive it well.

It's not always going to be sunshine and roses. My team knows I'm always going to be honest, no matter what, and I'll tell them if something isn't up to standards. But I'm just as willing to come back on the other side, be open about what I do like, and celebrate successes together in real time.

Assume the Best

It's so easy to get offended—just look at the global social, economic, and political climate we're living in. But that kind of thinking will never lead anywhere good. I'd much rather err on the side of grace. I live by the mantra of assuming the best while preparing for the worst. This way of thinking doesn't just apply to physical circumstances—it applies to your interactions with the people in your life too.

People ask me how I've developed such a thick skin. You have to be really tough to work in the business I do. You have to learn how to deal with rejection and inconsistency and change. If you can't find a way to process that, let it go, and move on, it will eat you up. The way I handle it is by assuming the best about people until they prove otherwise.

I have to practice this way of thinking a lot when it comes to email communication. It's way too easy to hide behind email, and because you can't see the sender's face or hear the inflections in their voice, it's easy to misinterpret. If I have any question in my mind about the tone of an email, I read it three times, then I pick up the phone or send a text and ask for clarification. Sometimes things are going on that I can't see, and they come across unintentionally in the email. Don't rely on just one form of communication. It's too surface-y. I always dig, because I like details, and I'm always eager to dive in and go deeper with someone. I guess that's just the scuba diver in me.

If you're the one sending an email, give it a quick read through before you hit send. Sometimes even something as minor as your mood can cause the tone to seem off. Maybe you're coming out of an argument at home and you haven't fully transitioned into work mode. It's normal to need a time of adjustment in a transition. Unfortunately, it's also common to have unspoken negativity seep into written communications. Keep your communication clear by taking time to process your messages and responses.

Follow Up

Open communication involves a back-and-forth exchange. Follow-up is one of the most important ways to keep your communication flowing. Pay attention to how well you follow up with others and also to the level of follow-up you receive in return.

First, I ask myself whether follow-up even occurred. Was there a phone call, an email, or even a text? Was my communication acknowledged? If it wasn't, then I have to ask myself why. Does the other person not know how important following up is, or do they just not care? Lack of communication is deadly. It's an immediate trust killer in any relationship, personal or professional.

Be an Open Door

I have an open-door policy with the people in my life. I want them to feel comfortable approaching me, because people are what really matters. So I've always worked hard to be the kind of partner, daughter, friend, and leader that people WANT to talk to, even if what they need to approach me with is difficult.

Part of what makes someone approachable is just being willing to have fun. Yes, we work hard. Yes, we jump into some pretty gritty and grimy messes. But the ability to have fun strengthens teams and helps burn off stress and strain.

I knew the exact moment I lost their attention. We were in Singapore on assignment, and it was our half day off for cultural immersion. We were out walking, and suddenly I realized several of my team members were focused on something off the path. When I realized what it was, I laughed.

"Oh my god! Have you ever done that? Let's go up there!" I said.

One of the men agreed right away. My team member Jeff was not so sure.

"No way, Rhonda," he said, backing away and shaking his head, his eyes huge. "I'm afraid of heights."

"Well, then," I tugged at his arm with a mischievous smile. "We're definitely going."

I marched them right up to the bungee swing and paid the fee. We all strapped in together, and I placed the ripcord handle in Jeff's hand—he could pull it when he was ready. And he did. The rush of adrenaline was amazing. I laughed the whole time. I think the guys were petrified, but we all still talk about it to this day because it was something fun we did together. That interaction bonded us as people, not just coworkers, and it opened up doors for communication about any topic—the fun ones and the no-nonsene, get-your-hands-dirty ones.

One member of my team, Gerry, has been with me through thick and thin over the last 18 years. But there was a short period of time when he left to work on another project. I understood. It was early on in our working relationship, and although we'd worked on a big project together, Gerry didn't owe me anything.

He quickly realized things weren't what he had hoped. Within three months, that company's leadership had lied to him about what was going to happen. That's when I got a phone call. He didn't beat around the bush.

"Rhonda, I'd like to come back to the team."

I was so glad he knew that he could openly communicate with me, even after three months away. I trusted this man with my life, so immediately I knew we'd find a place for him. I thought for a bit, then answered.

"Okay, sure. I have a position out at a data center in New Jersey. I want you to go out there and run that for me." Gerry had been working in Chicago while his family was on the East Cost. This move would bring him back to his family again—and I needed someone inside to watch the situation that was unfolding. I had a gut feeling that things weren't as they seemed in New Jersey, and if anyone could take care of it, Gerry could.

And he did. For two years, my guy worked closely with the head of that company. They were complete polar opposites, so I know it wasn't easy. He did it anyway, and he did his best to make them successful. When I was asked to go to London on a turnaround, I immediately called and asked him to come with me. At that time, I straight up told him, "Listen, I know you're keeping that company afloat. It's time to see if they can make it on their own. Sink or swim."

Gerry agreed to come to London with me, and we've been working side-by-side on assignments ever since. The executive in New Jersey didn't fare as well. Within six months, he was removed from his office. My team member really had kept that company afloat, and I was so glad he had reached out to me to get his position back. That took guts, a willingness to be vulnerable and communicate even when it was hard.

Gerry is one of my people, one of my top five. If the world fell apart, he's one of the people I'd want in my bunker with me. Who are your five? Who would pick up the phone if you called at 2 am? Find those people and cling to them for all you're worth, because they are the ones who will have your back no matter what.

Technology's Double-Edged Sword

Technology plays such a pivotal role in global communication today, yet it also has the potential to hinder our face-to-face inter-actions and even put our personal safety at risk. How do you address the safety concerns that come with communicating with someone you've never met who could be hiding behind a false persona? How do you balance the amazing ability to communicate across the globe with your responsibility to your own personal safety and face-to-face interactions with others who are right beside you?

Technology enables us to instantly communicate with people across the world who share our common interests. We can create global connections that can be so beneficial personally, professionally, and culturally because of email, messaging apps, and social media. The younger generations have harnessed this almost without thinking about it. It's completely normal for someone in their twenties or thir-ties to communicate with people halfway around the globe, making the world feel smaller and more connected.

Yet the anonymity of communicating online can also open up Pandora's box when it comes to security issues and personal threat. How do you know if someone on the other side of the screen is who they say they are? They could be an actor or someone look-ing to take advantage of you. There's a story in the news every day about a young person lured away by the false promise of an internet romance. There has to be a balance of face-to-face and online interaction.

Don't you hate it when everyone whips out their phones at a dinner party? Instead of candlelight, everyone's faces are backlit by the glow of an LCD screen. We need to be in the moment and enjoy communicating face-to-face with each other. The device can wait.

Although I do have notifications and reminders loaded into an on-line schedule app, I'm dedicated to my Tiffany-blue calendar. I need the physical calendar in my hand with the daily, weekly, and month-at-a-glance views. It's what works for me. So does having special time with my husband one-on-one. It's one way we show that we value each other, and it helps us avoid miscommunications about our plans.

You must know how to balance high-tech with high-touch. So take the technology out of the equation whenever possible. If you're only communicating via phone or email, you're missing out on the nuances of language and nonverbal cues that you get when you're face-to-face with someone. Put your phone down. When you're with someone, really be there with them. Not only does it make miscom-munication much less likely, it also shows the other person how much you value their physical presence and that you appreciate their contribution as part of your team.

FOCUS STATEMENT
I give and receive
clear and open communication.

8

RECOGNIZE YOUR TEAM

Give Your People the Red-Carpet Treatment

When my coworker walked into the room followed closely by one of the India team managers, I could tell he wasn't there to deliver good news. I don't think I'd ever seen Gerry look so grim.

"Rhonda, I've got bad news," he began.

I stood up a bit straighter and involuntarily clenched my fist. In my line of work, you tend to unconsciously brace yourself when those are the first words out of someone's mouth.

"One of the Indian team members died on a bridge call." He went on to explain that my team had been on a service call earlier that day with the company's team in India. There had been a power outage, and my team was working with theirs to help resolve it quickly. The gentleman in question had been on the call, and then suddenly he wasn't. No one could reach him, and after enough time had gone by, the local team realized something wasn't right. They called his mother to check on him, but he was already gone.

It crushed me. When I work with teams, no matter where they're from or what company they're with, those people become like family. This man had been a valuable part of our team, and I felt the loss deeply. Gerry motioned to the team manager at his side.

"We want to represent the company and be with his family at the memorial service," he said. And without hesitation, I answered, "Go. Do whatever it takes to get there."

Gerry and the team manager left within 24 hours, paying a premium price for last-minute tickets, but it didn't matter. They needed to be there. His family needed to know what a valuable member of our team he had been and how much we had appreciated him.

I wasn't able to go to India for another three months, and that weighed heavily on me. When I was able to return, I immediately sought out this man's family to express my condolences. I also let them know that the company had renamed a prestigious performance award after their loved one and asked if they'd be willing to present the award at the next ceremony. We were also able to present our team member's family with a gift of money that the organization had raised. As the former team member's father handed the next recipient this award, you could see the pride mixed with sadness on his face. I left India that trip knowing that respect and recognition had been given where it was due.

Every single person contributes to the overall wellness of an organization. A strong team is the key to growth, stability, and impact. Learning to recognize your people and appreciate how much each individual matters not only boosts your team members, but also makes you shine as a leader.

Everyone Has a Team

You may not work in a corporate environment managing teams of hundreds of thousands, but that doesn't mean you don't have a team. Look at the people around you, the ones you interact with daily. It doesn't matter how many are on your team, where they live, or what they do. They may be coworkers or fellow committee members or people in your circle of family and friends. Those people are your team, and they are important.

You're not an island. You will never accomplish as much on your own as you will as part of a group, so resist the temptation to go it alone. Working as part of a team isn't easy, but it's worth it. Opinions will clash. Ideas will differ. Sometimes you'll have a group of diverse personalities working together. And just because you're in charge doesn't mean people will agree with every one of your decisions. The important part is that you always come out the other side of a challenge having treated your team with the recognition they deserve.

Recognize the Person

Behind every position is a valuable person who makes an important impact on the bottom line. They're not just a means to an end. They don't exist to be a production machine. They're worthy of respect and recognition for what they do.

Consider a sports team. Each position is vital and plays a specific role. Take one position out, and the team is instantly weakened. But when everyone is operating together as a unit doing the things they're best at, the team does better all the way around.

People find it strange that I interact so closely with my teams and treat them like family. I find it strange that they don't. Why would you not want to honor someone who is in the trenches with you every day helping you achieve the business's goals?

I expect a lot. In fact, I expect top performance from all of my teams, both locally and internationally. But I recognize that as their leader, it's up to me to set the tone for our interactions. It's my responsibility to make sure they get what they need in order to succeed. If I don't know my teams—if I don't know who they are and what they do—then I'm not doing my job.

The reality is that I work for and with my teams. I'm not above them. They're not below me. We're working in it together. I need to know them. I need to know what they're thinking, feeling, and going through so I can meet their needs and they can do their job most effectively. And there are a few things I incorporate into my team interactions daily that help strengthen our connections and give them the kind of working environment they deserve.

STAY POSITIVE

Remember, you're the one who sets the tone. If you're slamming doors and throwing temper tantrums in the office, you're reinforcing that kind of behavior. You don't want a group of grown men and women mirroring that back to you. Even when things go wrong, take a moment to breathe and be grateful for your team. You can grit and grind your way out of this together.

BE THANKFUL FOR SMALL THINGS

I was raised to say please and thank you. I'm sure you were too. As toddlers, we parrot back these automated responses, but some-where along the line we tend to let that go by the wayside. The urgency of the everyday takes over, and it's easy to forget to express thanks and appreciation. It may seem like a very small thing, but it can make a huge difference.

At the end of the day, I don't want anyone putting their head on the pillow and going to sleep not knowing where they stand. They shouldn't have to guess. And honestly, expressing gratitude isn't hard. It barely takes any energy at all. Yes, if someone has really blown me away, I'm going to tell them how much I appreciate their efforts. But I'm also going to take some time to thank the person who sent me a file quickly when I was in a pinch.

I'm convinced that it's not always the one big accolade or ac-knowledgement that makes the most difference in people's lives. Sometimes it's the consistent, daily affirmations accumulating over time that build that trust and unity among your team. Those tiny little micro moments motivate them.

ALLOW THEM TO LEAD

This one can be tough. When you're a leader, it's easy to fall into the trap of thinking you're the one who has to be in charge all the time or that no one else can do it as well as you can. Well here's a spoiler alert for you—you are not the only one who can lead.

One of the best ways I can recognize my team is to allow them to lead. I don't mind stepping to the background and allowing someone else to take point when it's warranted. I'm always looking within my team for the next leader, the next person who could do what I do. I consider it an honor to train future leaders, and how can they learn how to lead unless I give them that freedom?

When people join my team, they recognize that willingness in me. I have team members who have followed me from job to job. They are loyal to me, we work well together, and much of the reason for that is because I step back and allow them to lead. They all have such amazing strengths. They're strong in ways I'm not sometimes. When that happens, then I'm doing myself and my team a disservice if I don't let them take charge.

PUBLICLY RECOGNIZE THEM

I also believe in publicly recognizing my team members. Not only does it build up the individual, but it also builds up the team as a unit. Watching each other get praised for their accomplishments makes them want to continue to do so for each other. It sets the tone for how you want them to treat each other. That's why I institute quarterly award ceremonies with the international teams. They don't have access to me as often as my local teams, so it's even more important for them to know that they're valued and respected.

Do you know all your team members? When you manage huge teams like I do, that can be difficult. There's no way I'm going to be able to personally know all of the thousands of members of the teams

I work with. But whenever I can, I make an effort to get to know as many as I can. Even just knowing their names makes an impact.

I'll never forget the time that I mentioned a backroom technician by name in a meeting. "What do you think, KB?" I'd asked. I watched as he swiveled his head around to figure out whether I was talking to him or not. When he realized he was the focus of my attention, he hesitantly lurched to his feet and gave a nervous yet competent answer. As I thanked him and gave positive feedback on his reply, I saw his whole demeanor change.

Up until that point, KB had been slouched quietly in the back of the room. He'd never been called on to contribute in a meeting before, never been recognized for anything he had done. This is so common. The leaders and managers tend to get all the credit while the entry-level team members fade into the background.

Over the next few weeks, I saw things change for KB. He stood taller and spoke up more. My public acknowledgement and encouraging words had built him up and validated his role in the company. He willingly spoke up more and offered solutions and feedback in meetings because he'd been shown his position was valued. All because I took maybe 90 seconds to show him I knew and recognized his contribution.

Imagine if you did that for your friends. Or your spouse. Or your committee members. What might happen to change your whole world... or theirs?

LOOK PAST THE POSITION

There's one thing that should be constantly in the back of your mind when it comes to your team. It's a question I ask. Am I looking past the position to the effect that company decisions have on their families? I encourage my leadership team to consider the people behind the positions as well. Everything that affects the employee is also going to affect their spouse or significant other and their families and children.

When an employee feels like you care about them and their family, they will care more about you and your company's goals. Their quality of work and engagement on the job will be better.

Because I work with multinational corporations, I usually have teams operating on multiple continents at any given time. Although we're separated by great distances, I still want to foster a team mentality and make sure the multinational teams feel connected. To accomplish that, I insist that all my teams are treated like family.

Servant Leadership

I'm not in this corporate world to be an empire builder. That type of management holds no appeal for me. I don't put myself before the people I manage. Full-contact leadership requires that you be right there, in the trenches, doing the hard things with the people on your team. I'll say it again: I work FOR my teams. How else can I expect them to work for me?

It's my goal to be the best leader I can be so my teams can perform to the highest level and tap into hidden resources they never knew they had. I want them to work through the challenges life presents. I want them to find the diamond inside themselves and not be afraid to go through the heat and the pressure to have it revealed. And I want them to know I'm in the bunker fighting right next to them. Because that's where the fun is! In the experience. In the journey.

Speak the Team Language

When you work with large global teams like I do, there can be a big learning curve on how to best relate to and communicate with team members. Even though it's a challenge, I believe in the small but fitting gesture. I like to recognize my team members in ways that appeal to them, even though that means individually assessing each one to find just the right method to use. For example, when I travel, I like to speak in the local languages, even if it's just a few phrases.

One resource I've found helpful is a book by Dr. Gary Chapman and Dr. Paul White's book, *The 5 Languages of Appreciation in the Workplace*. Drs. Chapman and White break down the ways people like to be appreciated into five main categories. Understanding which category your team member belongs in can show you exactly what would translate as meaningful appreciation to them.

- **ACTS OF SERVICE:** This team member feels most appreciated and recognized when you do something that helps them.

- **WORDS OF AFFIRMATION:** This team member thrives on positive feedback from others.

- **QUALITY TIME:** This team member wants to spend time with you face-to-face, talking and being together.

- **TANGIBLE GIFTS:** This team member loves to be recognized with small gifts like souvenirs from travel or a cup of coffee from the shop on the corner.

- **PHYSICAL TOUCH:** This language of appreciation isn't primarily a work language due to the personal nature of touch. But remember that things like a handshake or side hug can mean a lot to some team members.

Recognize Your Personal Teams

My professional teams are important, but my personal teams are the backbone and support of my life. I couldn't do what I do without my loved ones behind the scenes. They're just as much a part of my team as anyone, and the things we accomplish together as family, friends, personal staff, and mentors are the things that enrich my life to the fullest.

Don't forget to recognize the people in your personal life.

I think people who only know me at work would be surprised at the everyday Rhonda. I have a wonderful family. My girlfriend group and I are constantly in contact in a group chat that continues at all hours of the day and night. We keep tabs on each other. If we haven't heard from someone in a couple days, we check in. It's so essential to surround yourself with good people, and my nucleus is important to me.

I make sure my people know how much I value them. I'm a giver, not a taker, so I love sending personalized thank-yous and gifts. It's something I can do while leading such a hectic life, especially when I'm overseas.

And I spend a lot of time with my loud, Italian family. I learned to value the people in my life from my mother early on. I wasn't spoon-fed. I worked HARD for everything I've ever accomplished. And my mom was always in the background supporting me. She never once told me I couldn't accomplish something or that I should leave it to the boys. Want to know what she did tell me?

"If you want to do something, you go do it!"

She recognized the greatness in me. She complimented me when I was doing well. My mother gave me wings then taught me to fly, and I respect her so much for that. Recognition for her was spending time together. Growing up, we went to church every Sunday.

After church we'd go to the Kennedy Center to see a play or to the orchestra and have brunch. It taught me to respect tradition and doing things that maybe I didn't appreciate at the time. Those are some of my fondest memories. A little recognition goes a long way in your personal life too.

Recognition Results

Recognition takes time. It takes energy. It takes thought and consideration. But when you consider the rewards that you and your company reap by showing your team members how valued and appreciated they are, you AND your company win in a major way. Actually, three major ways. Recognition builds relationship, grows productivity, and instills loyalty.

What happens without recognition? You hate Mondays. You practice your inner pep talk in the mirror as you get ready for work.

"I can do this. I can get through this. Only five more days until Friday."

During your morning commute, you brace yourself to check your messages. You've been ignoring them since Friday night. You know you should really check them on the weekends, but you don't. You need a break, and the weekend is the only time you have to unplug. Sure enough, there are 17 messages from your manager waiting in your inbox.

A wave of anxiety washes over you. The only time you ever get emails over the weekend is when something has gone wrong, even if it isn't your fault. Looks like the week is off to a great start already.

As you scroll through your boss's messages, you think again about looking for another job. You love what you do, but you think you must not be very good at it. You never receive feedback unless you've done something the manager doesn't like, and you find you get less and less done because you're always spending time going over your reports before turning them in to make sure everything's perfect. You don't think you can take much more negative feedback.

The story could be so different if your manager gave you more positive feedback and worked to connect with you on a personal level. Your confidence would grow, and the whole working environment, as well as your attitude around it, would improve. Let's try that scenario again.

With regular recognition, you hum a pleasant tune while you sip your coffee and get dressed. First thing on your mind this morning was an amazing idea for your team's new assignment, and you can't wait to get to work to share it with your manager.

"She's going to love this! I'm so glad it's Monday."

You find your usual seat by the train window so you can watch the sun come up on your commute. Out of habit, you unlock your phone screen and tap to open your email. Five messages over the weekend from work. Your team leader always says not to worry about answering messages on the weekend—she'll call if there's an emergency—so there are usually several waiting for you on Monday. You really look forward to them.

The first message is the weekly schedule. You scroll quickly to the bottom and smile to yourself when you see the honorable mentions your team leader has added to the end of the schedule, as usual. Scroll, scroll, scroll...there you are. "Thanks for sticking it out for that extra fifteen minutes on the conference call on Friday. You're amazing!!"

The next email contains a funny GIF that your team leader knew you'd get a kick out of. You grin when you see it.

"I love my job. They'll have to haul me out when I'm eighty."

Do you see the contrast? In the first story, you feel unappreciated. The only feedback you get is negative, so you feel like you're always in trouble and your work doesn't matter to the company. You dread going back to work on Mondays, you often think about getting another job, and your productivity is falling because you're so concerned about making mistakes that you're taking twice as long to complete tasks.

On the other hand, we find a very happy you in the second scenario. You cheerfully look forward to going to work each week because your efforts are valued and appreciated. Your boss sends weekly messages with positive feedback for the whole team, which makes you excited to open your inbox. You don't mind working a little longer every now and then because you're invested in the company and the team, and you have no plans to seek a new position.

The second scenario perfectly illustrates the difference that recognizing your team can make. These concepts can apply to any kind of team you work with. It's worth the extra time and effort to show appreciation for the people in your life. It's worth it for their sake AND your own.

ALWAYS GIVE FEEDBACK KINDLY

Bad news can, and should, be handled gracefully. Put yourself in your team member's shoes. Criticisms are taken so much better when they're framed positively. If you have something not so great to share, make sure you follow up with some positive feedback. People can handle hearing what they're doing wrong so much better if they also hear what they're doing right. This also helps me create a safe environment where my team feels like they can tell me anything, anytime.

BE HONEST ABOUT WHAT YOU NEED

Your team doesn't know what you expect if you don't tell them. They aren't mind readers. Give clear expectations and don't be afraid to outline them multiple times or more than one way. It takes seven to eight exposures to information before things sink in and become memorable. So don't get discouraged if it seems like someone just isn't catching on to what you need. Just keep being honest.

MAKE TIME FOR FUN

Be willing to spend time with your team members outside of work. Sometimes I'll just ask one of them to lunch and we'll spend an hour or two just swapping stories and sharing what's going on in our lives. It creates a connection between us that goes beyond the job, and it gives us a chance to celebrate successes together in real time.

Recognize the Position

The companies I work with normally have end-of-year reviews, and they're kind of a big deal. Yet sometimes, I struggle to see the point. Why wait a whole year to recognize someone's accomplishments? I dive wholeheartedly into providing a thorough review, but I don't only do it once a year. A year is a long time, and I believe that my team member's positions deserve more recognition than three lines of "attaboy" on a form once a year.

People work hard, and providing valuable feedback for them is one of the most vital things I do all year. Recognizing the importance of each position validates the employee, energizing and encouraging them to continue to produce great work in that position. It benefits the whole company.

As I've mentioned, I often work with large-scale teams from overseas, and giving them recognition frequently is even more important—and effective—for them. We fly out and visit our international teams once or twice a quarter to give awards and recognition. I know for a fact that most managers would not do this. I will never stop doing it though, because it makes a huge difference in the culture and productivity of the teams. You learn early on what is happening on global teams when your feet are on the ground.

I'm a proponent of giving recognition when it is due—right then, in the moment—and here's why. If you wait and give out recognition just once a year, that means there were 11 months that your team didn't hear anything from you about how they're doing. That's just not often enough.

You don't have to have a huge ceremony every month to show recognition in meaningful ways. Sometimes it's the small gestures that really matter and make the most difference to your team members. I'm a big fan of sending thank-you notes or personalized emails. I'll also call the spouses of employees to make sure they feel cared for and appreciated.

FOCUS STATEMENT

I publicly and privately recognize the valuable contributions the people in my life make.

9

DISPLAY MANAGERIAL COURAGE

Dive In Without the Danger

It was the perfect day in paradise. We couldn't wait to spend the day on the ocean with nothing but sun, sand, and turquoise blue waters stretched out before us. I was vacationing in Cabo San Lucas on a trip I'd planned out a year in advance. We were out on a boat for the day when the captain pointed to a stretch of ocean near a rocky-faced cliff.

"*Cuidado!* Look for rocks." He pantomimed a wave crashing against the cliffs with his hands. I lifted up my binoculars and scanned the waters. As he maneuvered the boat closer to the cliff face, he explained how this area was commonly known for being a dangerous place to swim. Even the locals didn't swim here. I kept my eyes peeled, but I didn't see any signs of danger. The captain piloted the boat a bit closer to the sharp cliff faces and rocky outcroppings. I scanned the surface and peered into the depths, looking for any dangers in the water or rocks that sat too close to the surface. Everything looked safe.

With nothing to be concerned about in the water, I turned my attention to the cliff face. Instantly, I knew what I wanted to do. Before anyone could stop me, I stood up and dove over the side of the boat. I heard the boat captain shout just before I hit the water, but I didn't pause. I swam rapidly toward the rocky outcropping and, hand over hand and foothold by foothold, I climbed straight up the cliff face without a ladder. I turned around and waved at them cheerfully from the top—only one broken nail! When the boat captains and guide realized what I intended to do, they began frantically gesturing and shouting for me to come down.

"No, *señora!* No jumping here. It's not legal." The boat captain motioned for me to climb back around the cliff and get back in the boat. By that time, some of the locals including the dive master, Marco, had joined me. I just smiled and yelled, "Honey—take a picture!" and dove in.

I popped up out of the water, laughing and none the worse for wear, and Marco dove in right after me. I'd completely scoped out the area. I knew I could do it. There was no danger of injuring myself on a rocky outcropping. No sharks to be seen. I'd had plenty of time to consider the idea as I climbed up the cliff face, and my gut told me I should go for it. As I swam over to the boat, my husband looked up from his phone.

"I can't believe it," he said. "I missed it." He groaned and slapped the phone against the palm of his hand in mild disappointment. So of course, I immediately turned around, scaled the cliff, and did it again.

That time, he got the picture.

The Difference Between Carelessness and Courage

It's easy to mistake courage for carelessness. Many people will read that story and think, "Is she nuts? You don't just go cliff diving in Cabo."

They're right. I would never encourage anyone jump into shallow, rocky ocean. I completely respect that the sea holds mysteries and dangers. But I also trust my gut and my observation skills. I love adrenaline, but I'm not foolish. I grew up diving and swimming. After fully assessing the situation, I made the decision to jump in and do something I'd always wanted to do—cliff dive.

There are definite hallmarks that differentiate carelessness from courage. These help identify which side of the coin you're dealing with in others—and yourself. And yes, you do have to gauge this in yourself. Remember Sensible Rhonda and Full-Contact Rhonda? Without the balance that Sensible Rhonda provides, Full-Contact Rhonda would go headlong into danger just for the adrenaline rush.

Full-Contact Rhonda stared up at the rocky cliff face and said, "Now THAT looks like fun," while Sensible Rhonda countered with, "Yes, but have you done the work to ensure you're not just going off the deep end here…literally?"

Learn to listen to that back-and-forth in your gut.

CARELESSNESS SEEKS ATTENTION.
COURAGE SEEKS ATTENTIVENESS.

People who are careless often act recklessly to get attention. The more reaction they can provoke, the bigger the risks they're willing to take. Carelessness insists that all eyes focus attention on them, and they rarely, if ever, think of how their actions affect others.

In contrast, those who are courageous put the work into assessing a situation before acting. They don't go into things blindly, and they're more concerned with whether or not they've read the situation right than what everyone else thinks. They make decisions with others' needs and safety in mind.

CARELESSNESS SEEKS SELF-INTEREST.
COURAGE SEEKS STRATEGIC GAINS.

A careless person looks out for number one. They make choices that badly affect others without even thinking about it. As long as they come out on top, they don't give much thought to the outcome of their decisions.

A courageous person makes decisions and takes action based on well-thought-out plans. There's always a reason behind the choices they make, and they act for the good of the team, not just themselves.

CARELESSNESS SEEKS EASE.
COURAGE SEEKS ELEVATION.

A careless person loves the path of least resistance. They make snap decisions based on what's right in front of them. Researching other options and putting energy into weighing their options takes more time and investment than they're willing to make.

A courageous person is willing to do the hard things and sacrifice their own comfort to do what's right. They willingly forego the easy path in favor of the one that will bring the most benefit to others.

The Courageous Manager

But Rhonda, how can I display managerial courage? I'm not a manager. I don't have a team.

Sure you are, and yes, you do.

Managerial courage can be displayed in any area of your life. Trust me, even if you don't have a corporate or professional team, you're still managing a team of some kind, whether it's a committee, club, friends, or your family at home. You can display managerial courage no matter what your life looks like by diving into the grit and grind around you. So what does managerial courage look like?

MANAGERIAL COURAGE STICKS UP FOR
WHAT'S RIGHT

Corporate offices are kind of like little closed communities. You're with the same people day in and day out. You get used to the rhythm and cadence of the place. And you can tell right away when something out of the norm has happened, because everything in the atmosphere changes.

It was Mother's Day, and the moment I walked into the office, I knew something was going on. The air was tight, and small groups of employees were clustered around watercoolers whispering and murmuring to each other. When I tried to make eye contact, they scurried back to their desks. Just as I was getting ready to head to another executive's office and ask what in the world was going on, I got the notification.

Meeting in Conference Room B in 10 minutes. Ooooookay. I changed direction midstride and headed for the conference room.

"Rhonda, we have an issue," said one of the department heads. He didn't beat around the bush as he explained that one of the male employees had come out as transgender and had arrived at work that morning in a dress. I blinked. That was kind of unusual for a Mother's Day at 7:00 am. Right away I got a sinking feeling in my gut. I knew what was coming next, and I was not going to be okay with it.

"We want you to fire him," he said.

I took a deep breath and thought for a moment. The executives in the room were in charge of the corporation. They had hired me and they could fire me, but the hiring and firing that took place internally was my call.

"Is it affecting their work performance?" I asked, looking around the room and making eye contact with each person. Each gaze wavered, then fell. Good.

"Well, no but—"

"Then I won't fire this employee," I stated firmly, then walked out. I went up against Human Resources and the legal department. I knew firing them would be wrong, and my moral compass wouldn't allow it no matter what kind of pressure they put on me. A top performer and loyal employee did not deserve to get fired just because they bucked the status quo.

I won't lie to you though, it was one of the most unusual days I've ever spent in a corporate environment. Nobody knew what to make of it—one day this employee was showing up as a man, and the next they were arriving in a dress and heels with makeup and nails wanting to be called "Trisha." I knew standing by her was the right thing to do, but that didn't mean I wasn't going to deal with some issues surrounding the situation. Within the hour, those issues were at my office door in the form of a dozen or more male employees.

And they were losing it.

"Rhonda, you've got to let him use the women's restroom. He…she… she went in the men's room and tried to use the urinal in a dress," one panicked employee said. They had NO idea how to handle this.

"Guys, listen. She's a top performer. Trisha does her job. I don't care what anyone's gender or identity or whatever is. As long as some-one is doing their job, there's no reason to freak out. I'll take care of this." Full-Contact Rhonda was raring to go, ready to go to battle. But Sensible Rhonda won out. I needed to know what was going on with this person.

I knocked on her cubicle and heard a subdued, "Come in." I don't know what it's like to go through that kind of personal turmoil about your identity, but we sat down and talked it all out for over two and a half hours in my office. We came up with a way to make the situation work well for everyone, and she stayed with that company for more than 15 years.

I risked my job in that situation. But even if I had gotten fired over it, I would never be sorry that I stood up for what was right.

MANAGERIAL COURAGE LEADS PEOPLE THROUGH CHANGE

Change will come. A true leader steps up and leads people through change, even when it's hard. Especially when it's hard. People look to leadership in hard situations, and the quality of that leadership sets the tone for how change will be handled.

What kind of tone do you want to set?

Do you want to give in to the temptation to grow negative and resentful, creating an atmosphere of discontent and unhappiness?

Do you want to let fear and anxiety take over, leaving your team feeling uncertain and insecure?

Or do you want to hold your head high, dive into the grit and grind, and learn your way out of the mess? Because that's what full-contact leadership does, and I know you can do it too.

MANAGERIAL COURAGE EMBRACES THE MESS

When everything seems like it's falling apart, there's one thing you still have control over—yourself. You get to choose how you react.

You can push the panic button and run around yelling that the sky is falling.

You can lie down, pull your blankets over your head, and give up.

You can abandon ship and leave the mess for someone else to deal with.

You can run and hide and pray you'll still be kicking when it's all over.

Or you can roll up your sleeves and get your hands dirty. Tackle the mess, learn as you go, and create your own way out. You always have a choice. And that is powerful.

MANAGERIAL COURAGE KNOWS WHEN TO TAKE THE MOUNTAIN

Managerial courage doesn't make things easy. You'll have to make the hard decisions. And you'll still have questions.

How do you know when to go all-in?

How do you know when the results will be worth the risk?

You must have a process for weighing the situation and determining when the risk will be worth it. I process mentally when I'm training. The silence when I run or swim is my thinking time. But some people process verbally or on paper, and that's good too.

So many people get tied to the immediate. They can't see beyond the problem. They only see the problem and it's crushing them. How do you know you can do it? By remembering you've been through this before. Even if it's not the exact same set of circumstances, you've been in the midst of everything falling apart and you came out okay. You know the steps to handle it.

Risk vs. Reward Assessment

Here's an easy way to assess risks and rewards so you can move forward with confidence and take that mountain in front of you. This assessment is very simple. It takes just a few minutes to do, and it gives so much clarity. When you're in the heat of a situation, it helps you objectively weigh the situations so you can make a clear decision without letting emotions and feelings get in the way.

- **STEP 1:** Identify the problem. What's the situation you're dealing with? Lay it all out there.

- **STEP 2:** Write down possible solutions. There are always at least a couple options you can consider. One of the solutions might be to take no action.

- **STEP 3:** List the risks for each solution. If the risks seem overwhelming, just take the top 10.

- **STEP 4:** Assign each risk a value from 1 to 10, with 1 being the least impact and 10 being the greatest.

- **STEP 5:** Objectively make an assessment based on the risk factors.

Now that you have each risk laid out in front of you on paper in black and white, it loses some of its emotional power. Sometimes you realize the big scary thoughts rolling around in your head were unfounded and the risk wasn't really as high as you thought. Other times you get a dose of reality and realize there's more risk involved and you need to reconsider.

For example, let's say you've been unhappy in your current position for some time. You don't make enough to support the dream that you and your partner have of starting a family together, and you're beginning to feel trapped and hopeless. Then you see something in the newspaper that you can't get out of your mind.

Help Wanted. You circle it in red ink. The position sounds like your dream job. You email the contact in the ad right away, and sure enough, everything right down to the pay seems like a good fit. Everything, that is, except for the location. The job would require your family to move three hours south, away from your families and friends and away from the little home and neighborhood you love.

On the other hand, you've also been eyeing a potential promotion you see on the horizon within your own company. One of the executives one step up from your position will be retiring next month. You can't be sure, but all signs are indicating that corporate has its eye on you for the position—you're just not sure when the position will be available. How long should you wait? What should you do? Instead of letting worry and fear take over, you decide to take a different tack.

You and your partner sit down after work that night and fill out a Risk Vs. Reward Assessment. As you write down and rate the risks, you start to calm down. Interviewing for the position in the advertisement would require a move if you got the job—but at this point you haven't even interviewed. You realize you've been trying to cross a bridge you haven't even reached yet. Plus you'd be moving to an area with a higher cost of living. You quickly crunch the numbers in your head and realize that what seemed like a big pay raise at first suddenly doesn't seem all that great, especially when factoring in the lack of support from friends and family.

As you and your partner gaze at each other across the table, you know the decision has been made, and without all the agonizing you'd expected. You will stay, and tomorrow at work you'll schedule a meeting with your retiring coworker. It was about time you put 100% into getting the promotion within your company. You have a good feeling about it. And most of the time, that's all you need to move forward.

MANAGERIAL COURAGE SHOWS GRACE UNDER PRESSURE

The unexpected will happen. Plan on it. In fact, you should have a Plan B and Plan C. If Plan B is needed, so much can depend on your ability to keep a cool head in unpredictable situations. A huge part of that is being able to make difficult decisions fast in a crisis. (I follow a quick process that I outlined in Chapter 4: listen, process, and react.) Staying positive is important. If you go into a situation expecting a good outcome, you're better prepared to handle whatever comes your way.

In the middle of a crisis, your body experiences a surge of adrenaline. You can use this biophysical reaction to your advantage. Let it crystallize your focus and propel you. Follow your gut with a level head. Your sensible side will keep you on the right path, and your full-contact side will give you the drive and courage to push through. You've prepared for this. You've got the experiences behind you and the battle scars that prove you can handle it.

I've experienced catastrophic events firsthand on more than one occasion, one of which will live in the minds of Americans everywhere. They will never forget where they were and what they were doing the day the Twin Towers fell. There's no way you can plan for something like that. When you hear something so horrible, so beyond the scope of anything you ever dreamed would happen, it's your instincts that carry you through. The patterns of behavior you've nurtured in yourself every moment up to then will come out.

What will come out in you? Will it be strength of character? Tenacity? Honesty? Hope? Or will it be panic? Despair? Bitterness? Apathy?

I've watched grown men try to throw themselves out of windows when they realized they'd lost everything. I've had to shake the hands of parents who lost their son on a job site I oversaw. And I've crawled on my hands and knees at Ground Zero, fiber-optic cables in hand, with life literally falling down around me in a haze of soot and ash. Those are the moments you find out what you're made of. Don't fear them. You can't stop them or prevent them from coming. Embrace them for what they can teach you, and use them to push you onward.

MANAGERIAL COURAGE DOESN'T BACK DOWN

Here's the truth—sometimes you won't FEEL very courageous. But we all start somewhere, and even little acts of courage add up. Every time you take one step and then another, you're building your strength of character. Each decision and choice you make prepares you for the next one, and looking back you can draw on those experiences, reminding yourself about what you've endured this far, and have faith that you'll get through this time too.

So many people get get tied to the immediate. They can't see beyond it, so they only see the problem. And it can crush them if they allow it. You've been through difficulty before. You know the steps you can take to handle it. You ARE courageous. I know you are. It's inside you. Sometimes you have to mine deep for it. Sometimes you have to experience the hard stuff before you start to see the courage show. But it's there. Don't give up. Keep going.

And don't forget—even if the outcome isn't what you hoped it would be, there's still reward in being courageous. If you put forth your all, persevere, and never give up, then you've won. You've become the kind of person people follow. You've become the kind of leader people will run through a brick wall for.

FOCUS STATEMENT
*I will have managerial
and life courage.*

10

KNOW YOUR METRICS

Calculate the Risks and Come Out On Top

We stood at my desk, looking down at a brief. I'd seen more serious situations, more dangerous situations, more dire situations...but I don't think I'd ever seen something quite so complicated. Whoever took on this contract would have a massive task in front of them. In the hands of a team that wasn't prepared to do what it took to turn things around, the corporation wouldn't make it, and thousands of people would lose their jobs. The workload would be insane, the pressure intense, the expectations high—and all within a very short time frame. I tapped my manicured fingernail on the brief's cover sheet and slowly lifted my head to meet my team member's gaze.

"Well," he said with a half smirk, "looks like we've got our work cut out for us on this one."

I smiled. The decision was made. From that moment, it was on. Over the next few weeks, my team and I completed a detailed assessment of the environment and performed a full request for proposal. We were tasked with selecting an outsource partner and moving everything over to them. The transition had to be complete within 24 months, or the corporation would face an insane financial penalty.

Within nine months, we had a contract in place, and implementation was completed well within the time frame with no significant negative impact to the business. We also re-platformed the entire company to run on a single, global standard operating procedure and engineered a cheaper hardware solution that reduced a nine-hour task to one hour. Talk about fun!

People thought we were crazy. No one expected us to get results like that going in. The whole situation looked like a disaster waiting to happen, but I knew it was possible. I knew what our team was capable of accomplishing together and how long it would take us. The support team around the industry was and continue to be rock stars. From there, it was just a matter of reverse-engineering the process from finish to start, setting up benchmark goals, and making a timeline. There was no "I think we can do it" or "I guess we'll just see if it works." I KNEW it would work, because we ran the metrics. You can't manage what you don't measure or monitor. Call on your nucleus. You're all on the journey together.

Results-Driven Livin'

When it comes to the way you live your life, you have two choices. You can sit back and let life happen to you. These people are content to let life happen to them. They're reactionary, and never really take action on their own. I'm all for being flexible and ready to pivot with whatever situation the Universe throws your way, but there's a big difference between holding things loosely and holding on to nothing at all.

That's not full-contact living. People who live full contact are re-sults-driven. They don't wait around, content to just react. They take action and do what needs to be done. But what makes them so sure of themselves? What gives them the confidence to make big goals and then go for them?

In the previous chapters, I've given you the blueprint to building the kind of full-contact foundation that will energize every part of your life and reveal your true mettle. You've learned about the impor-tance of being prepared, listening first, recognizing your team, and all the rest...and all of those are important. But it's this last princi-ple—know your metrics—that gives you the confidence to live a results-driven life of action.

Does that sound intimidating? It shouldn't. I guarantee you're living in results-driven ways right now without even realizing it, and I can prove it to you. Even normal, day-to-day tasks require knowing your metrics. If you can apply this principle to the small things in your life, you can apply it to the big things. So...want me to prove it to you? Here's an example of results-driven action from my own life.

I'm training for a race right now. My training schedule tells me that tomorrow I need to be in the pool by 5:05 am to swim laps. And yes, 4:30 am is early, but I'll be up and out the door by then because I want to be ready at the starting line when the gun goes off, and I'm willing to do what it takes. I'll be going to bed early tonight, and before I turn the lights off, I'll make sure my gym bag is packed with everything I need for my workout. I've got chocolate Muscle Milk waiting for me in the fridge, so I'll grab that on the way out in case I get hungry. Traffic will be light that time of the morning, so if I leave by 4:45 am, I'll be diving into the pool at 5:05.

- **DESIRED RESULT:** To be prepared and well trained for the triathlon next month

- **GOAL:** Be in the pool by 5:05 am

- **KNOWN METRICS:** How much sleep I need before a training session, what I need to bring with me to the gym, how long it takes me to get to the gym

- **UNKNOWN METRICS:** Whether I'll be hungry before/after the workout

I can confidently say I'll be in the pool by 5:05 am tomorrow morning because I know my desired result, I've set a goal, I've considered what my known metrics are, and I've addressed any unknowns. Now I'm ready to make a plan that will help me achieve my goal (my workout) and ultimately get me my desired result (ready for the triathlon).

See what I mean? I barely gave that any thought. My past performance gives me the confidence I need to take action, because I know that when I've followed this training regimen before, it's been successful for me.

Now think about your own life. Pinpoint an area where you're already practicing results-driven livin', then reverse-engineer it like I did above. The beauty of this is that you can apply this same strategy to the really big, important areas of your life. It works, and just knowing you're already doing this in your life with success is such a confidence builder.

You look at the calendar and start to panic. Your flight to Beijing for a conference leaves in five days. There's so much to do before you leave. You can't even think about packing or preparing for your presentation yet. Then you stop yourself. *Yes, I can.* You decide to set aside your lunch hour to plan out the next few days so you can board the plane feeling confident that you're prepared and ready. Lunch hour rolls around, and with your turkey wrap in one hand and your pen in the other, you begin writing out your plan.

- **DESIRED RESULT:** Board the flight to Beijing in five days feeling cool, calm, and collected

- **GOAL:** Arrive at the airport two hours early with everything I need for the conference

- **KNOWN METRICS:** Pack, arrange for transportation, get a good night's rest beforehand, check in online, google the news in Beijing, and print my boarding passes

- **UNKNOWN METRICS:** I won't know how long the airport security lines are until I arrive. Look into TSA precheck to see if I qualify. Build in extra time in case traffic is heavy.

You put the pen down feeling much better. There's nothing on that list that's unmanageable. You're ready to make a plan to spread out what needs to be done over the next five days. You've got this.

Be a Go-Getter Goal-Setter

Full-contact living means purposefully taking action to achieve the goals you set. But how come we're so often our own worst enemies when it comes to setting goals? Do you sit back, hesitant to take action because you're not sure how big is TOO big? Or maybe you reserve your goal setting for New Year's resolutions that never get met. Guess what—that's completely normal.

Be kind to yourself. By all means, go all-in and take action—no one else is going to do it for you—but also be practical about it. Rome wasn't built in a day. Goal-setting needs to be done on a weekly basis to keep the goals manageable. Transformation and metrics-building takes time.

"But Rhonda, I don't even know what metrics means for me yet. I'm really not sure what I'm capable of."

That's okay. Everybody starts somewhere. The important thing is that you START. So let's break it down. Metrics are basically just measurements or a string of proven results. If you want to start building some metrics into your life, start by deciding what your desired results are then work toward achieving them.

In the example above, my desired result is to be ready and well trained for my upcoming triathlon race. Being in the pool by 5:05 am tomorrow is just one of the small goals that will help get me to my desired result. By focusing in on the small daily goals, I'm not as easily overwhelmed. I just focus on accomplishing the next one, and the next, and eventually I will arrive at the end result.

You can do that too. If you feel you don't have much in the way of metrics to gauge yourself and your results by, then search for ways you can build more experience into your life. Let's say you want to start being seen as more of a leader in your community. There are things you can do right now to help build up your metrics.

GET YOUR FOOT IN THE DOOR

First of all, ask for opportunities that will get your foot in the door. Decide which skills or deliverables you want to be known for, then get out there and start asking people if they know of opportunities for you to grow those skills. If there aren't any paid leadership roles available, look for unpaid ones. Volunteer for a local charity. Serve on a board or committee. All these experiences are so valuable because they provide practical experience even when you're just starting out.

SHOW UP, STAY VISIBLE, AND CONTRIBUTE

Next, stay visible in the public eye. The more you show up, the more people start to automatically associate you with someone who's out there leading, taking action, and getting things done. Speak at a local banquet. Attend public events. Get involved in your sphere of influence and make a positive impact. You've got to get yourself out there and let people know who you are and what you're doing.

START SMALL AND WORK YOUR WAY UP

Finally, take even the small jobs. Small opportunities still get you visible, and they can lead to bigger ones down the road. I started out as a junior lifeguard when I was 13. That was my first job. If you hold out for that one big thing, you're missing all the chances along the way to learn and grow through the process. Don't underestimate the power of starting at the bottom and working your way up. Work for what you want. That's right, get out there and earn it.

Avoid Setbacks While Setting Goals

If you're going to go full contact, it's time to step up and embrace goal-setting. Goals are absolutely necessary because they help you break down a project into manageable sections to work toward. That doesn't mean goal setting is easy. In fact, the moment you start setting goals, I'm guessing you'll start getting some internal, or external, setbacks. I'm going to address the four most common setbacks that keep us from making the kind of results we were meant to achieve.

FEAR IS A LIAR

The first goal-setting setback is fear. It's easy to set goals that don't push or challenge you, but you're capable of so much more than that. That's why I'm going to let you in on a little secret—fear is a liar. Don't let it keep you from what you're meant to do or the person you're meant to become. Trust me, Sensible Rhonda tries to talk me into playing it safe all the time, but I don't let her win. If you're purposefully avoiding goals or are setting goals that you know you can easily meet because you're too afraid to fail, you'll never get the results you want.

In October 2018, I participated in a 55-mile run across the Singita Grumeti Reserve to support women's empowerment. The reserve is a 350,000-acre stretch of land in the middle of the Serengeti in Tanzania. Guess what lives and roams freely there? If you guessed lions, you'd be right. The first time I saw a pride of lions lounging nearby during the run, I was extremely appreciative of the armed guards who had accompanied us. The event had over 100 armed guards keeping us secure from predators and poachers, and I was so thankful to have several guards—Helen, Edward, Johann, and Edward—with me at all times.

It's one thing to see lions from a safe distance at a zoo or from a safari Jeep. It was an entirely different experience knowing I was running across their home turf on open ground with nothing between the number one predator in Africa and me but the watchful care of armed guards. Lions can run faster, jump higher, see better. I found myself praying, *Please don't let me look like lunch. Please don't let me look like lunch.*

As nerve-wracking as it was to be in that situation, I wouldn't have missed it for the world. I trusted the guards who accompanied us runners. I know they would look out for us and keep us safe. My job was to run and bring awareness to women's empowerment in that part of the world, and I made bonds with the other women who ran. Elana, Lisette, India, Katherine, Bessie, Marietta, Alina, Michelle—these are the women I'll never forget. Full-Contact Rhonda would never let me panic, bail on the run, and hide in the safety of one of the Jeeps.

TEMPER YOUR EXPECTATIONS

Oh, expectations. Expectations can cause major setbacks when it comes to goal setting. If Sensible Rhonda errs on the side of fear, Full-Contact Rhonda goes all out with unrealistic expectations.

"So what if that goal is totally unreasonable or unattainable. Who cares if doing this would cause more problems than it's worth. Never say die."

Calm down there, Full-Contact Rhonda. I'm all for taking risks, but they need to make sense in the overall scheme of things. Setting goals that are completely unreasonable and unattainable will only discourage you and make you want to give up. They're just as bad as setting goals that are too easy.

MY DOG ATE MY HOMEWORK

The third setback to goal setting is lack of good research. Make things easier for yourself by researching your goal before you commit to it and with your current responsibilities and schedule in mind. Yes, you'll need to put in a little time on the front end, but in the long run, you'll be so glad you did. Instead of going in blind, which is something I never recommend, you'll have a base of knowledge that will help you every step of the way as you work toward the goal. Research helps you avoid overcommitting to something you currently don't have time or space for in your life. It also helps you set goals that make sense for you in regard to your abilities so you can harness your strengths and skills to achieve them.

DITCH THE DOUBTERS

People say you are the sum of the five people closest to you. If you're having trouble setting and sticking to your goals, you may want to check your network. Do they doubt and criticize everything you do? Belittle the goals you strive for? Seem uninterested or even hostile about your lifestyle? Are they unable to set and achieve goals themselves? If so, it might be time to find a new tribe, and this time look for people who will stand beside you and have fun with you, people who are trustworthy and loyal. I couldn't accomplish anything without the support and expertise of my team, family, and friends.

Chase the Goal With Focus

I do all of my training in silence—no phone, no music, nothing. Most people think that's crazy. They ask me how I keep from getting bored. The truth is, there's no way I could ever get bored when I'm training because this is my active meditation time.

I tune out external distractions. This is the only time when I unplug from all tech—no cell phone in the pool or the treadmill—and completely, totally focus on letting my mind order things subconsciously. I need that downtime, because it allows me to decompress. I think things through and strategize. I develop solutions to problems and situations in my work. I also take time to just be. I listen to the birds, the sound of the traffic on the road, horns honking, and I watch the sun come up.

There's no right or wrong way to meditate. It just depends on what works for you. Some people can practice resting meditation, but I've found that I think and process best when my body is active. When I'm swimming laps or running, I hit a cadence where my body and breath are in rhythmic motion and my mind is freed up to process thoughts more clearly. Then my natural intuition takes over, and all my best ideas and strategies come out.

Take this time away from your regular day-to-day activities. Do something that lets you really zoom out and see the situation as a whole. This will allow you to create a plan within the framework of your metrics. Then you can zoom back in and focus on the goal with laser-like intensity. Because you're building the goal in the framework of your proven metrics, you don't have to question whether you can do it or whether it's a good fit. You'll already know before you even put the goal out there.

From Milestone to Milestone...and Beyond

The phone rang one Sunday morning at 11:30 am. "Rhonda, we need you in the office ASAP." The voice on the other end sounded strained. "How quickly can you get here?"

I got the call that one of the largest investment banks in America was going bankrupt about 48 hours before the news channels picked it up. I immediately called in the team, and we were on site within an hour. There was nothing we could do to save the situation. We were there to mitigate as much damage as we could and ease the transition, but there was nothing "easy" about it.

When the news hit the media, we were all holed up in one of the main offices—you know, the kind where it's all glass windows and cubicles with rows of desks. It was over. Employees started to trickle in to gather their things and empty out their offices. They had just found out they'd lost everything they had worked for their whole professional lives. I'll never forget the shell-shocked, despairing look on some of their faces.

There are some things no amount of training can prepare you for. One executive picked up an office chair and ran full speed at the window trying to break it so he could throw himself out of it. It had just sunk in that he'd literally gone bankrupt right along with the company. No severance pay, no 401K, and no job.

Everything in his life had been tied to his position with the bank. Everything. He didn't have any other goals. He hadn't put any new milestones in place, because he thought he had arrived. He had his desired result, so somewhere along the way, he'd quit making goals and dreaming dreams and pushing to grow and improve and take action. When his milestone sank underwater with the company's bankruptcy, he was left adrift, because he didn't have another milestone to pivot to. He didn't have a Plan B.

The unexpected happens. You have to be ready with the next thing. People ask me all the time what I'm going to do next, and I always have an answer. When you meet a goal, don't just stop and rest. Move on to the next milestone. We should always be learning. When we stop learning, we stop growing. There has to be a "something next." We ALL need more milestones on the horizon. That's why I say grit and grind is a practice. You never stop.

You Can Do More Than You Think

When the plane touched down on the runway after a birthday trip to Africa with my best friend, Michelle, my mind was already a day ahead of me. I navigated through the airport, threw my carry-on into the trunk, and let my driver take me home. I then drove from Connecticut to Maryland for the 70.3-mile Eagleman Ironman, a race with a difficult swim leg people refer to as swimming in the "chop tank." In less than 24 hours, I'd be lacing up my running shoes, and I was looking forward to the drive time so I could mentally prepare.

Make no mistake about it, I was exhausted. Jet lag is a beast. But I hadn't spent hours running across the Serengeti to keep up my training for nothing. I had made it up the four-mile incline at the St. George race earlier in the year. If I could do that, I could do this.

I don't run these races to win. Although I know what my times are for the races, I don't run for time. My goal is simply to walk away from a race knowing I finished strong and did my best. And I turned in my personal best time during that race.

I could have turned down the Eagleman Ironman. No one would have blamed me. I was just coming off a 32-hour journey. I was jet lagged to the max. I was barely going to make it there in time, and I was going to be running on very little sleep. Surely there would be better races to run. All of those reasons made sense, but I knew I could do it.

You can always do more than you think you can. When you come to the end of what you know you can take, there's always one more reserve. Who cares if people think you're nuts? When you succeed, they'll change their tune. Leverage what you know you can do to get one level further than you did the last time. Plan ahead and put measures in place that will help you make sure you can do what you set out to do. You're not going it alone—you have a team behind you, remember? Don't be afraid to ask for backup when you need it.

That's how I knew I could do the Eagleman race—I planned ahead, got the support I needed, and drew on strength from my past experiences. I ran through the Serengeti often during my trip to Africa so I could be ready for the Eagleman race. That wasn't an easy thing to arrange, but I made it work. I booked a first-class ticket for my flight home so I could sleep on the plane and get the rest I needed before the race. I made arrangements to drive myself to Cambridge so I could have the silence and stillness of the car ride to mentally prepare and process the Africa trip and work.

Know Your Metrics

There's so much power in knowing your numbers. When you've done your research, prepared for every possible contingency, and drawn on your past results, your team will far surpass anyone else out there. You have a competitive advantage over other teams because you're willing to do the work it takes to know your numbers BEFORE you go into a situation.

Knowing your numbers...

- Allows you to do things people say can't be done.

- Enables you to act faster than anyone expects.

- Equips you to succeed where others have failed.

- Helps you manage your bottom line in business.

- Means you're always aware of your profits and losses.

As I've said many times before, you can't manage what you don't measure. You can't fix problems that you don't know about. The funny thing is, I had to learn this one the hard way when it came to training for races. For a long time, I didn't bother to track everything or set training goals. When I first started, I just signed up for the ones I thought looked fun without taking into account my work schedule. I paid for that in stress and strain, let me tell you. But I learned from it as well—I pivoted to a better training system, paying closer attention to my work schedule and planning my races more effectively. My results helped me pivot so I could succeed.

TRACKING PERSONAL METRICS

There's a difference between how you track metrics for your personal life and your professional life. With your personal life, you're tracking your interactions with the people you love most and how you prioritize and allocate your time with them. When it comes to my personal metrics, I have a Tiffany-blue calendar that I use to record everything. I track how many times a year I see my mother, my family, my friends. I plan all my races and training schedules out. Everything goes on that calendar up to a year in advance, so I can make sure I don't miss anything important. It's a necessity for me to do that, because I travel over 200 days a year on average for business. I don't want my family and friends to feel like they got the short end of Rhonda, so I'm very purposeful about it.

As busy as I am, I also need to build rest into my schedule. I do take breaks. I say no to stuff all the time in order to protect my personal life. Remember, every time you say no to one thing, you're actually saying yes to yourself in a different way, and that's good.

There are definitely things I don't keep track of though. Some of my friends keep asking me to download a running app called Strava. Strava allows you to track the distances and times of other runners on the platform and meet up on runs. They really get into it, but I haven't joined, and I don't plan to. I'm sure it's great for runners who are competitive about their times, but I'm not. I don't train for time. I train for preparedness and fitness. I train so I can finish a race knowing I did my best. If I downloaded the app and started trying to keep up with other runners and compare myself to them, it would completely sideline my training.

When I say know your metrics, I don't mean every single metric there is. There is such a thing as TOO much measurement. You have to learn to separate out the really important ones for your goals and focus on those. Don't get bogged down by details that aren't relevant for your end result, especially when it comes to your personal life.

TRACKING PROFESSIONAL METRICS

Conversely, you can't track too many metrics when it comes to business. I have a huge team to help me with that, but it's my responsibility to always know what they are and be on top of what the metrics are showing. I personally track people I promoted and how many people have advanced or moved within the organization. People are what really matters, so I take that as my personal responsibility. I want to make sure I'm helping my team members' careers however possible. One of the worst things that can happen is for team members to get stagnant. I don't want people to stand still and get too comfortable, so I move them around. If the people in an organization aren't thriving, then its bottom line won't thrive either.

I also keep close tabs on the finances, and I'm very strict when it comes to the results. In technology, I always shoot for 100%. If tech goes down, there's no room for error. Even 30 seconds can make a difference, like when someone needs money from at ATM to feed their family, so I overshoot everything in that arena.

With business metrics, I think in terms of tracking outcomes. I set the outcome—the end result I want to see happen—then I work backward and reverse-engineer all the goals and benchmarks from there. In order to do this, you must have reliable metrics from previous experiences. So I also track progress as we move forward. Are we meeting the benchmarks? If not, is it because we need to work harder or because we had bad metrics to work from? The more data you have, the more accurately you can predict what needs to happen for success.

Be Ready to Pivot Fast

Not everything you do will be a blazing success. Don't be afraid of that. In fact, I think it's so beneficial. Some of the most important growth lessons take place in failure, because it teaches you how to pivot, and pivot fast.

How do you know when it's time to pivot? Watch your metrics. If you've done the research and background work you need to before diving into an assignment, you have those numbers right in front of you. When you put in the time on the front end to know what good looks like, based on experience, intuition, and the numbers, you'll be able to catch any downward trends quickly. You'll have benchmarks already in place. Because you already have this information, you'll identify when change is needed right away and be able to pivot faster than anyone else.

You Are NOT Your Metrics

Sometimes people ignore their metrics because they identify a little too closely with the numbers. They feel that they ARE the numbers. If the metrics are too low, that means they are a failure. If the numbers are high, then they have to fight hard to keep them there. It's the reason some people don't like to balance their bank accounts— after all, they can't be out of money if they still have checks left!

Here's the thing—metrics are only tools. They're simply a part of your toolkit. You use them to uncover trends. Metrics can show you whether you're heading in the right direction or if you need to change some things around. They can show you where you may need to apply more heat and pressure. They can tell a story about the past.

But the metrics are not a reflection of who you are as a person. The more you can dissociate yourself from the numbers, the more you'll learn to love them as the tools they are.

Metrics are the Glue

Knowing your metrics is like the glue that holds all of the other principles together. How? When you know your metrics...

- You can be well prepared for almost any situation.

- You recognize how much time you'll need to accomplish your goals. That, in turn, helps you value others' time.

- You can listen to hear and understand instead of frantically thinking how to respond when someone asks you about your processes or results.

- It's easier to hold yourself accountable. You know what results you're going for and exactly what it will take to achieve them. You're less likely to overpromise and not be able to follow through.

- Honesty comes naturally. You have nothing to hide, because your metrics are something to be proud of.

Knowing your metrics helps you succeed and grow in all the other principles. When you know your metrics, you have measures you can use to continue to push yourself to grow. They show you when you need to work harder. They show you when it's time to regroup and pivot. And they can also show you when it's time to take a break and give yourself grace.

Knowing your metrics gives you the confidence to take risks. You can dive into something that's a mess even if you don't know how you'll get out of it, because your metrics tell you what you're capable of, which resources you have at your disposal, and what you'll need to see it through.

Finally, tracking your metrics isn't something you ever finish doing. Living a full-contact life is a process of continual refinement. Keep going until you take your final breath. Look for that next milestone, and don't be satisfied with good enough when you know you could have more.

FOCUS STATEMENT

I make it a priority to know where I stand professionally and personally.

11

INVEST IN MENTORSHIP

**You Don't Know Everything,
But You Know a Lot**

So you've learned about the 10 principles, but I have a bonus one for you. When I graduated from college and entered the professional world, one of my first professional mentors was named Sam. I had no idea at the time how important my relationship with him would become.

Sam and I worked together in telecommunications at the beginning of my professional career, and it took me a while to get used to his style of leadership. The things he said didn't always make sense to me.

"Rhonda, you need to learn how to play golf."

"Seriously, Sam? No. I don't have the patience for it, and it doesn't even feel like I'm exercising,"

"You have to do it," he insisted. "A lot more than just golf is accomplished on the golf course."

I didn't listen. Golf was the LAST thing I wanted to learn how to do. In fact, it's only recently that I learned to play it. And I have to admit that he was right. I didn't believe him all those years ago, but executives tend to talk about business issues and plans on the golf course, things they would never discuss in a boardroom.

I didn't listen to Sam about golf, but he was my president, so you better believe my ears were peeled when it came to his direction on the job, even if I didn't understand it. You see, Sam had this habit of moving me around. A lot. Every two years, he would pluck me out of the division I was in and plop me right down in the middle of another one.

I didn't get it. What the heck? I would just get things to the point where I finally had everything ironed out and running smoothly in the division I was in, and he'd come along and switch me to another division that was in even worse shape. I finally sat down with him one day and got gut-level honest.

"I don't know anything about this stuff," I complained. "I didn't go to school for this." I had no idea why he was doing this to me. I felt like I was being punished for something, but I didn't know what I'd done wrong. I'll never forget the answer he gave me.

"You went to school. You have managerial qualities. Plus, you have great instincts and the ability to lead people," he said. "Don't you see? I'm moving you to the messes."

Gee, thanks...I think? I didn't fully understand what he had done for me until I left the telecom field and moved into finance. Finance is a huge, intense field. My first move was to apply for a position as the managing director during the merger of two of the world's largest banks, and I didn't think I would get it. Everyone saw me as the underdog—underexperienced, underqualified, and under 30. But because Sam saw potential in me and trained me to seek out and take care of the messes, I got the position and became the youngest female managing director in the finance industry at that time.

To this day, I am grateful for all of his support. When I realized that he had prepared me for everything that was to come in my professional career, I went directly to him and asked the question I should have asked in the beginning—the question he'd already answered with his actions.

"Will you be one of my mentors for the rest of my life?"

Why is Mentorship Important?

From the moment we're born, we experience mentorship at its very basic level. As infants, we couldn't speak, walk, dress ourselves, throw a ball, or sing a song. We were fed and cared for by parents and caregivers who did all those things for us until we were strong and cognizant enough to learn how to do them for ourselves—and then they taught us how. The older we got, the more we could accomplish and figure things out for ourselves until we were fully functioning adults living out in the real world.

That's how deep our need for mentorship goes. So why do we ever stop seeking it out? Maybe we don't need to keep learning basic life skills anymore, but that doesn't mean we should stop learning. The stakes are even higher for us as adults. The lessons are bigger and more pivotal. We need to connect with people who know more than we do and have been there and done that. No app, course, or podcast can teach you in the same way that person-to-person mentorship can. It's irreplaceable.

You will never be so smart, so accomplished, or so advanced that you won't benefit from learning from someone ahead of you. And the good news is, there's always someone who knows more than you on any given subject. Why not learn from someone else's experience and apply it to your own life?

Choosing a Good Mentor

Choosing a mentor is a decision that should be considered carefully. This person is going to become an important part of your life. How can you make sure you're selecting the right person?

CHOOSE SOMEONE YOU CAN TRUST

You're about to invite someone to shape parts of your life. Make sure it's someone who will be discreet, who will guard the information you share with them. You don't want to hear things you've said in confidence repeated back to you by someone else. By definition, mentors help you figure out the places you're vulnerable and insecure, so you also have to trust that they will take the relationship seriously and not take advantage of your weak points.

CHOOSE SOMEONE WHO FITS
YOUR MENTORSHIP NEEDS

Before you choose a mentor, consider what you want to be mentored in. The more specific you are on what you want help and guidance with, the better your results will be. If you have a problem controlling your temper in boardroom situations, look for someone who is always cool, calm, and collected no matter what goes down in a negotiation. If you need advice on parenting, find the best mom you know. Want to become a better public speaker? Find someone who speaks a lot and ask them to share all their secrets with you.

CHOOSE SOMEONE WHO'S BEEN WHERE YOU ARE

Find someone who has walked the path you're on. They will understand the pitfalls and challenges you face and be able to empathize with what you're experiencing. There's power in knowing you have someone in your corner who's been there, done that, and come out the other side.

CHOOSE SOMEONE FURTHER ALONG THAN YOU

This one seems pretty obvious, but I've seen all too often what happens when people at the same level advise each other. Without the depth of experience and knowledge that a more seasoned person can bring, a mentorship is simply a friendship. Friendships are so valuable, but they're not the same as mentorships. Choosing a mentor who's further along can provide you with important wisdom and guidance on how you can reach that level yourself. You can't get that from someone who's at your level or below.

CHOOSE SOMEONE WILLING TO CHALLENGE YOU

Mentors do more than just listen. A true mentor also advises and challenges their mentees. They're not afraid to ask the hard questions, and they don't hesitate to hold you accountable for your actions, help you create benchmarks for your goals, and then insist that you stick to them. You want a mentor so you can grow, not just be given a pat on the back. You can get that from anybody.

CHOOSE SOMEONE YOU LIKE

When you were a kid in school, which teachers did you learn the most from? Who were your favorite instructors—the ones you had a special connection with, who invested themselves in your lives, and who showed they cared? We learn better from people we like and respect. Spending time with them is easy, and we get more out of our experiences together because positive emotion connects us.

Mentorship isn't a magic wand. It's a relationship, and relationships take work. You can't just show up, chit chat, and expect all their knowledge and experience will be automatically transferred to you. Be proactive about what kind of experience you want this mentorship to be. Come prepared with questions. Be clear about your goals and hopes. And above all, choose wisely.

How to be Mentored

If you choose the right mentor, you've just opened up an amazing opportunity to learn from someone in a way that reading a book or listening to a podcast can't provide. Nothing replaces the face-to-face or voice-to-voice personal connection of a mentorship for helping you grow and make progress on your journey. But the mentor can't pull the weight of the whole relationship on their own. To get the most out of the mentorship relationship, you as the mentee have a responsibility to engage as well.

FIRST THINGS FIRST

Don't be afraid to ask someone to be your mentor. Put some effort into the request so they can see you're serious about investing in the relationship. You'll also be setting a tone for the level of investment you're hoping for from them. So just do it—ask. In today's world, people don't like to ask for help. That's why the words "Will you be my mentor?" are so powerful.

There is a wrong and a right way to ask. I recommend making a personal, face-to-face connection with that person. Don't just spring a request on them suddenly. Trust me, it won't be received well. I get email requests like that all the time. In fact, I got this one just the other day from a total stranger.

> Good morning, Rhonda,
>
> I hope you're enjoying your summer. This summer I ended up getting an internship with the golf club for the Masters. I've been working on a marketing campaign to promote an inaugural golf event that'll be played during the next year during the Masters. During my eight weeks there, I worked very close to a well-known agency working on PR marketing projects. Although I enjoyed my time there and learning about the business, I'm hoping to find an internship with you next year. I'll be an incoming junior in college, and I'm studying marketing. I'd appreciate any help or advice that you could give and love to work with you on your team.
>
> Hope to hear from you soon.

This email just put the cart three miles ahead of the horse. I don't know this person. We've never interacted before. There's no way I'm going to just hand out internships without some kind of connection with them first. Create a relationship, give a compliment, start a conversation—there are a million ways to do something that's of value to someone before asking for something in return. Put in the work to make a good first impression. A random email is not going to work. At best, it gets ignored. At worst, you just annoyed a busy person who has no desire to help you.

COME PREPARED

When you know you'll be meeting with your mentor, take some time to prepare. Research the topics you want to discuss. Write down any questions you'd like to go over. Review your notes from the last session and tie up any loose ends or assignments they gave you. Be ready to grow more and more each time—expect it. When your mind is open and ready to receive what your mentor says to you, you'll make progress quicker and in a more lasting way than if you were to get defensive or distracted.

BE OPEN

Go into your meetings with an open mind that's ready to learn. Your attitude is under your control. You can choose how to approach the appointment. It makes a huge difference. Life will always throw the unexpected at you. It's your job to be ready so it doesn't sideline your time with your mentor.

Scenario 1

You rush into the room 10 minutes late, stressed out and already on your last nerve. On your way over, you realized you'd forgotten your house key and had to turn around and go back. You hate being late, and suddenly the appointment seems like just one more thing in a long list of things to do today. When your mentor comments about your tardiness and asks if everything is okay, your defenses instantly go up. *She doesn't know what my morning was like. How dare she judge me for being late!* Your focus is gone, and you barely hear a word she says the rest of the appointment. You leave wondering why you even went in the first place.

Scenario 2

You rush into the room 10 minutes late. On your way over, you realized you'd forgotten your house key and had to turn around and go back. You hate being late, but you take a moment to breathe and let the frustration go. You don't want your crazy morning affecting your time with your mentor.

When you arrive, you hug and explain what happened. You laugh together as she relays a time when she thought she lost her keys in a Walmart parking lot, only to find them 45 minutes later nestled between the canned corn and the dried pasta in one of the shopping bags. *I'm so glad I'm here. She's so understanding.* You continue with your appointment together, and you come away with some action steps to implement throughout the week.

See the difference? Your attitude matters, especially when things go wrong. Another aspect of being open is being willing and ready to do the work. Your mentor is not just going to hand you solutions. That's not their job. They'll give you guidance and support, but it's your responsibility to figure things out and work toward the solutions you seek. Your mentor isn't a genie. It's not an instant gratification situation. Show up with a positive attitude and put in the work to make the relationship productive.

FOLLOW YOUR MENTOR'S ADVICE

You've done the groundwork and chosen a mentor based on the principles above. Now it's time to get down to the grit and grind. It might not always be easy, but if you want to become the best version of yourself, it's time to dig in, do the work, and follow the advice your mentor gives you. This is why you have invited them into your life.

When I was working my way through college, one of my professors encouraged me to take a job with a telecommunications company. My knee-jerk response was to say, "Oh no. I don't do that. That's not what I've studied. I don't know that industry."

He replied, "Does it matter? Look at the job description. Can you communicate well? Yes. Can you lead? Yes. So what's the problem?"

That moment with one of my first mentors taught me not to be afraid to go for every opportunity to try different things and take positions that challenged me. It was the start of my obsession with milestones as well. I wanted to prove to myself and others that I could rise to a challenge and succeed.

Be a Mentor

The beautiful thing about mentorship is that anyone can mentor someone. It's not a one-way street, and it's not an either-or situation. You can be both a mentor to one person and a mentee to another. Just as everyone needs the guidance of someone richer in knowledge and experience, there is someone out there who can benefit from what you have to offer too.

No matter what level you're at right now, you've been where someone else is standing—and struggling—right now. You have experience and wisdom that can help them get through. You are the person they need!

Being a mentor is one of the most humbling experiences in life, and that's why I think everyone should do it. It means you give of yourself and invest in others. It's a sacrifice of your time, your energy, your emotions. There's definitely some grit and grind involved. And it's absolutely something every one of us should do for others.

You don't have to be an expert. You don't have to be a super high-level executive or Nobel Peace Prize winner. There's really only one thing you must have as a mentor: willingness.

How to Be a Good Mentor

Investing in another person's life is one of the most important things you can do. At the moment, I am mentoring several younger women as they navigate life and career changes. I take my responsibility as a mentor very seriously, and I have a very close and trusting relationship with each of them. The relationship is what makes mentorship work.

Being a good mentor takes purposeful, conscious effort on your part, but don't be afraid of that. Mentoring the next generation one person at a time is one of the most worthwhile and rewarding things you'll ever do. Plus, they're not the only ones who benefit from the relationship. Being a mentor sharpens you, and you end up learning a lot about yourself in the process.

PRIORITIZE APPOINTMENTS

Make the appointments with your mentee a priority. If you've committed to invest in their lives in this way, it's essential to be consistent and present in the relationship.

LISTEN FIRST

Listening is your main responsibility as a mentor, and the way you listen is important. Your mentee deserves a well-thought-out answer. First, listen to hear and understand, then process and respond.

BE HONEST

Honesty and trust are the basis of your relationship. Just as you expect honesty from your mentee, they should know they're going to get the same in return. Don't hesitate to call them out if you see something that needs to be addressed. They've invited you into their lives, and you want them to learn and grow. Be intentional with every single piece of feedback you give. Everything can be a lesson if they choose to take it that way.

BE CLEAR

Set up any boundaries or limits you have right up front. Sit down and outline what your relationship will look like, when and where you'll meet and for how long. Share expectations about what form of contact is acceptable. Hopefully these are just formalities, but it's important to establish guidelines at the outset to head off any unrealistic expectations before they happen.

The next generation needs you, as the General, one of the people I look up to the most told me. In fact, he gave me the push I needed to write this book. Our culture is changing so fast. Human interactions are becoming less frequent. Social media and technology create a false sense of connection. I know that sounds strange coming from someone who makes her living managing technology every day, but it's true. Technology is a tool. It can connect people in the basic sense of the word, but it can't create true connections. Creating a genuine connection is something only two people can do.

Be willing to be one of those people.

Types of Mentorships

Sometimes a mentorship lasts a lifetime. Other times it meets a need in a certain season of life and runs its course. And then there are times when you bring this type of relationship to an end because it just was not a good fit.

Lifetime mentorships are some of the most valuable, precious relationships on earth. Parents and caregivers are our first lifetime mentors, but throughout your lifetime you may encounter others in different areas of your life who can fill that role as well. Hallmarks of a lifetime mentorship include consistent growth and engagement, a beneficial atmosphere for both parties, and shared life and goal directions.

Seasonal mentorships happen more frequently. They usually occur over a shorter period of time, months or even a few years, and exist for a more focused purpose in the mentee's life. A new mom might have an older mom as a mentor while her baby is still at home and she's in the day-to-day grit and grind of caring for an infant. In a few years though, her needs will change and she may think about moving back into the workforce as her children spend more time at school. That early mentorship will always be a precious one, but she may now want to transition into a different mentorship that matches the new stage of life she's in.

Know When to Move On

Sometimes mentorships just plain don't work out. Timing and logistics can play a role. Maybe one party moves away, or there's an emergency in the family that pulls their attention elsewhere. Other times, a mentorship ends because the personalities of the parties involved don't mesh well. This happens, and it's okay. Do not feel guilty about looking elsewhere if a relationship isn't working out.

As a final word, protect yourself. If at any time the mentor you've chosen makes you feel unsafe, threatened, harassed, or belittled, leave that relationship. That kind of treatment is not okay in any relationship, and you deserve better. Be willing to make the hard decisions and have the tough discussions when it seems like something is off. Trust your gut.

FOCUS STATEMENT
*I will seek out trusted mentors
and offer my mentorship to others.*

CONCLUSION
Grit, Grind...and Diamonds

Grit and grind starts right where you are. It takes place every day, sometimes little by little and sometimes in more intense waves of pressure and heat. The important thing is that you're here. You're showing up.

By now, you've read through all 10 principles (and the bonus one on mentoring) and have learned how putting each one into practice can help you live an all-in, full-contact life. You've been encouraged, over and over again, to jump into whatever life throws your way and to learn your way through it. If you implement what you've read, it will have a profound effect on your life.

How profound? You'll be changed right down to your very core.

I won't promise you it will be easy, because it won't. There will be times along the way that you'll wonder how much more you can take. You'll feel like you're going to crack under the strain. You'll reach the end of yourself and fear that the stress will completely wear you away, so there's nothing left.

And in some ways, that's exactly what will happen. If you continuously push yourself to do the hard things and subject yourself to the genuine grit and grind of life, you'll be fundamentally changed. You may feel like everything you were has been worn away. The heat and pressure of life does take a toll, and when the ash clears, you may not recognize what's left—but that's not a bad thing.

Why? Because when something is repeatedly exposed to heat and pressure over time, it becomes something infinitely more brilliant, pure, and valuable.

A diamond.

The Making of a Diamond

The principles in this book are meant to be lived together. They're not stand-alones. You can choose to start with one or two and work your way through them from there. That's a good strategy so you don't overwhelm yourself all at once. But you can't just stop there. To get the best results and reveal the extraordinary diamond you are inside, you need the strong foundation built by all 10 working together.

The full-contact lifestyle encompasses everything from your relationships with yourself, your family, and your friends to your professional life and how you build and manage a team to how you interact and connect with the world outside. If you're weak in one area, it affects the other areas too. Thankfully, it's a process. It takes more than heat and pressure to make diamonds—it takes time too. Go at your own speed. Don't listen to the naysayers and those who stand on the outskirts criticizing and passing judgment.

Run YOUR race.

Pressure Is A Privilege

If you're really going to embrace the mess and learn to thrive not just survive, you have to accept the idea that pressure is a privilege. It's not something to be avoided or endured. If you build your whole life around avoiding the hard things and circumnavigating stressful experiences, you're not only selling yourself short on what you can accomplish, you're also denying yourself times of growth that will make you a stronger, better person.

Remember how I told you my mentor used to move me from position to position every two years early in my career? I was so frustrated by it at first. I didn't understand why he was telling me to go into industries and areas I wasn't experienced in, most of them in highly male-dominated fields. Looking back, I can clearly see how that benefitted me. I would never trade those experiences for the world, and I'm so thankful to my mentor for his wise guidance, because it's given me decades of milestone experiences to draw from.

Think about the events in your life that have produced the most growth in your character. It wasn't the easy-street, happy-go-lucky, smooth-sailing times when you accomplished the most growth, was it? No, the times that taught you the most and produced the most strength and maturity were the ones that had the most challenges and pressures. Would you change them? Given the chance, would you choose to go back and not experience them if it meant you'd have to leave the newfound growth and strength behind?

I don't think so.

Because I know how badass you truly are!

Don't get me wrong—dwelling in the past never helped anyone, and that's not what I'm suggesting. What I am proposing is that you take what you've learned and use it going forward. These experiences you've been through can help you get through the moments of uncertainty and doubt that pop up when the next mess lands at your doorstep.

When you've walked through the fire and emerged on the other side once, you know you can do it again. And when you know you can do it again, you've already won the battle in your mind. Going in with a positive outlook makes all the difference.

So recognize when you're diving into a mess, and celebrate when you've made it out. The mess doesn't last forever.

Have you ever tried to help a butterfly escape from its cocoon or a bird emerge from its egg? What happened? Nothing good, right? The butterfly and the baby bird NEED that struggle to strengthen them to be able to survive in the outside world. They won't make it if they're not allowed to go through the ordeal on their own.

We humans are much the same. The struggle we sometimes see as something negative to avoid or escape is the very thing that makes us strong. If we refuse to dive in, take risks, and be willing to go through the grit and the grind, we'll never reveal the diamond hiding inside us.

Every time you tackle something head-on, you raise the threshold of what you know you can handle. By refusing to run screaming from the challenges in life, you're building character and a foundation that allows you permission to fail without being crushed.

Failures happen. Everyone fails sometimes, and there's nothing wrong with that. It doesn't mean you lost; it just means you tried and found a path that didn't work. Now you have a choice. You could sit down in the ashes and refuse to try again. *I've failed. That's it for me. I can't do it.* Or you can hop back up to your feet and pivot quickly. *Well, that didn't work. Let's try something else.* The old saying is true: you only fail if you quit trying.

You might be tempted to think you're not brave enough, that maybe you don't have what it takes. Baloney. Everyone has doubts. Everyone is afraid sometimes. You don't have to take on the whole world at once. You just have to take one step in the right direction, then another, and another. Always stay in forward motion. It's so much easier to adjust your course when you're already moving than it is to prod yourself to action when you're standing still.

The mess is there. The unexpected happens. It looks different for all of us. My mess might be a tense negotiation session halfway around the world, while yours could be a war with health professionals over medical treatment or as a soldier fighting in actual combat.

Embrace the mess. It's there whether you want it or not, so you might as well be part of the solution. Face it head on and take the initiative needed to act, even when you're scared. Especially when you're scared.

You've got this.

You're A Diamond

Psst. Want to know a secret? You've already made it!

You're already wildly successful.

The only thing we have in this life is this exact moment. And in this moment, you are perfect. You're here. You've arrived. You're whole.

No matter what your circumstances are right now, no matter how much of a success or mess you feel like your life is, those are all illusions. You might feel like an unshaped lump of coal, but that's not who you really are. Deep inside, you are a perfect diamond ready to be shaped in any way YOU see fit.

Everything we've talked about so far...those aren't things you have to find. You don't have to go out and GET them. You already HAVE them. They are inside you already. They don't cost any money. You don't have to be some kind of superhero. All you have to do is choose to use them to navigate through the rest of your life.

Be on time.

Be prepared.

Be accountable.

These are all states of BEING. You can't go out and buy "metrics." You can only choose to KNOW your metrics.

If you wait for circumstances to be perfect before you act, you'll forever be frozen in place. It's human nature to always desire growth and expansion, so by default, we can never be completely satisfied with the way things are. Circumstances will never be perfect. There will always be another mess to dive into.

Know what that means? There will always be situations with challenges to learn your way through. You'll always have another chance to keep refining and revealing the beautiful diamond inside you.

Isn't that wonderful?

The circumstances in your life that you don't like, the things you tend to avoid, the things you'd like to change—those are all life's beautiful gifts to you. They offer you a playground to grow and change and improve. It's your choice.

You can choose to view life as something to be endured, or you can choose to see it as a grand adventure, to be experienced in all its glory—the easy stuff AND the hard stuff.

The truth is, grit and grind is a practice, not a process. It's about constantly striving for that next thing and knowing you can do it. There will be failures. You won't always be prepared. There will be times you don't listen, you show up late, or you shrink back from managerial courage. And I want you to know that it's okay. A perfect track record isn't required. What matters is that you're constantly growing and following these principles as closely as you can from moment to moment. You never reach the finish line (until you're dead)—it's a continuous refinement. A daily practice.

So dive into the mess. Go full contact.

Love every minute of the grit and grind.

Enjoy the fact that you get to screw up, make mistakes, swim with the sharks—and that you'll be just fine in the end.

And rely on that internal structure—those 10 principles—as your guidance system. When you know your foundation is strong, you can trust yourself.

And never forget—you're a diamond.

ACKNOWLEDGMENTS

AUSTIN ADAMS: Thanks for believing in me and mentoring me early on. I appreciate all of the encouragement and advice.

BRAD ANDERSON: Thanks for the kick-butt interview in the Rolls-Royce. That was so down-to-earth and fun. So glad it was a hit!

MIKE BAILEY: Thank you for your lifetime friendship (since sixth grade)! I'm proud of the man you are today and how you're pursuing your dreams with Bret Michaels. You give it your all on the drums and in your life daily.

PAUL BARRETT: Thank you for coming up to me after speaking on a panel at GMU. Thank you for seeing the talent in me and recruiting me for the Longwood Advisory Board. I appreciate your belief in my ability to help in the education world. I'm grateful for all of the support.

MICHELLE MADISON BENOIT: You've been my best friend since we were three years old. We've been through everything in life together. You are my sister, and I wouldn't be who I am today without you in my life. Thank you for all of our quality-time exotic adventures. I love your children, Camille and Nico, with all my heart.

SCOTT BENOIT: You're an amazing dad, friend, and husband to Michelle. I admire all you've done in your life. I'm so grateful that we can always talk sports and have a blast together.

GERRY BERG: Thank you for being by my side all around the world for more than 18 years of working together. We have been in so many situations that we dug ourselves out of by being together. I wouldn't be alive without you—literally. Thanks for saving my life.

KERRI BREED: Thank you for always being there, checking in when I'm traveling on business, and being tuned in to the world news. You're the first to welcome me with a home-cooked meal. (And you know everything I like!) Thank you for all the warm welcomes.

MICHAEL BREED: Thanks for leading the way with innovation and re-branding, and not being afraid to jump into the unknown and lead. I appreciate that you're always trying new ideas and grinding it out.

GENERAL JAMES CARTWRIGHT: Thank you for being the inspiration, guiding light, and anchor in my life, for being my mentor, and most of all for your friendship. I treasure that friendship beyond words. You're in my bunker for life. Thank you for giving me the final push to write this book.

CHERYL CASONE: Thank you for your friendship, love, and support—and for coming into my life. Our long hour lunches and talks about every topic make life better. Here's to swimming with more sharks and pigs in Exuma, Bahamas.

DENISE CLARK: Thank you for your guidance and friendship, and for teaching patience...not to mention climbing the Great Wall of China with me, and our celebration at the top!

SASHA COHEN: From one global woman to another, I treasure our grounded friendship and our overseas adventures. I am so blessed that we met through Team USA. From the moment we met, I knew we would be friends for life.

KELLY COLE: You were right there outside my office with your dog Zeus when Lehman Brothers was falling. You're always there for me no matter how messy it gets at work. Thanks for being a fabulous fashionista and sister at heart.

KATHERINE CONAWAY: Thank you for always grinding all of the details out with me. I appreciate your eye for detail.

OWEN DAVIDSON: You always check in and give me grounded advice. Only words of wisdom come out of your mouth. I respect you for the man you are, not just your discipline on the tennis court.

VERONICA DAY: A true powerhouse who knows what she wants as an athlete and in life. I love being with you and can't wait to see what the future brings.

MICHAEL DELL: Thank you for supporting me in business and for always doing the right thing in support of the customers.

JAMIE DIMON: You always challenged me on details. Thank you for showing me the importance of knowing every number to the cent. You always ask the best questions, and that shows how much you truly care.

JIM DITMORE: Thank you for believing in me through the transitions to many companies. You are a true leadership professor, and I still learn from you daily.

JULIE EASON: My publisher and extraordinary everything. Thank you for encouraging me through this entire book process, helping me to tell my story, and for all of the amazing support. When you answer the phone with "Hello, beautiful!" it instantly makes me smile.

CAROLYN EDGAR: Thanks for the willpower and your skill in the art of negotiation. We've spent a lot of long hours together. I appreciate you grinding out every word in a contract.

ELANA, INDIA, MARIETTA, LISANNE, BESSIE, ALINA, KATHERINE, AND MICHELE: Thanks for running 55 miles through the Serengeti together and being the first women to do it. We have bonds for life.

KEITH GABEL: Your snowboarding prowess is amazing! I so admire your personality and how you focus on what you want in life.

LAUREN GILL: Thank you for being my publicist and helping me through everything in life and more. We've been through so much together, and it is a pleasure to have you as a true friend.

DAVID GOULDEN: Thank you for always being there to help in any way—whether in business or friendship. We have worked through so many items and found the solutions in the trenches.

GRACE, PETERLIUS, AND MY FAMILY IN SINGITA, AFRICA: Thank you for being my second family in life and for having hearts of gold. You all treasure life and work so hard. You have all changed my life.

JOY GREGORY: Thank you for all the love, support, and friendship, and for always making me laugh no matter what is happening.

DARYL GREEN: Number 28, RESPECT. You are one of my biggest sports heroes!

HELEN: The one and only female guard in Tanzania. You guarded me for multiple runs through Africa and remain in my heart daily. You grind it out in the trenches every day and protect everyone with a smile.

TOM HENDERSON (HENDIE): Thank you for all the laughs and for always reaching out and helping me stay grounded.

JAY HILL: Thank you for allowing me to focus on my career and life aspirations, even though it meant sacrificing family time over the years. You always have a sense of humor no matter what is happening. I appreciate your love and support, and I am so blessed by my three stepchildren who have become my friends.

STEVE HILTON: I love that we were promoted to managing directors together at JPMorgan Chase and have come full circle later in life to work together once again.

COBI JONES: You are an inspiration, showing what dedication is all about on and off the field. I respect you so much.

CVK: We've been through endless negotiations in business and countless hours of grinding it out. I'm grateful for the support and friendship that came out of tough times in the trenches.

SAM KAPOOR: You told me that I needed to play golf in my twenties, and I wish I had listened sooner. I am forever grateful that you took me under your wing and forced me to move around outside my comfort zone.

ELAINE KWON: Thanks for inspiring me with all your discipline, focus, hard work, and dedication in the martial arts. You're an amazing concert pianist, teacher, and all-around badass. You grind out every second of your day.

ROB LABRITZ: Thanks for making golf fun and most of all for your friendship. That swing of yours!

WILLIAM LAUDER: Thank you for all of the support at Estée Lauder Companies.

CHRIS LEWIS: Thanks for all of the laughs and deep conversations while playing golf at Winged Foot, for being my constant golf caddie, and for putting up with me. I treasure all of our summer laughs! You make my life better!

HIEU LUU: You were the brains behind so much technology and so many companies. Thank you for allowing me into your life and for becoming such a true friend during AIG and so many other crises. There has been a hole in the world since you passed. I miss you every day.

BRENDAN LYNCH: Thank you for all the caring support, friendship, and problem solving we've done together across multiple companies. You're always willing to dive down into the mess and fix the issues. You are an anchor, and I admire you for your daily hard work and for always combing through every detail.

AUNT MARGARET: You instilled the value of hard work in me at a very young age as I watched you become one of the first female lawyers on Capitol Hill in Washington, DC. Thank you for taking me to church and the Kennedy Center every Sunday so I could learn to appreciate culture.

ROBERT MASON: What else can I say? You are timeless. And you have the all-time best rock voice in the world. I admire how you've reinvented yourself and how much you believe in wellness while performing concerts on the road. You're a pillar of strength and friendship. "Who is my cherry pie" has so many meanings. Stay golden or stay platinum—I love those words! They mean deep ambition to me.

MIGUEL: Thank you for getting me from Point A to B safe and sound every day, no matter what state or country we're in.

MOM: From the moment I was born, you instilled the values of working for our rewards in life. Nothing was handed to me—you made me work for it. Thank you!

NEETI AND ARJUN: Thanks for traveling the world and completing digital transformation together with me. All of those airplane miles and meals! Thank you for always getting your hands dirty and grinding out the details with me.

NUSRAT: Thank you for always making me feel comfortable behind the camera. And for being the best photographer in the industry. I think the world of not just your artwork, but more importantly, your heart.

RACHEL, TARA, MICHELE, CHRISSY, KELLY, MICHELLE, AND DIANA: Thank you for the daily messages and checking in, and for keeping up the daily foundation of friendship with each other. Red tent!

CHRIS RILEY: You are so genuine and down-to-earth, and you're always solving problems. I admire how you bring out the best in people and surround yourself with the best!

JASON RIZZI: Thank you for getting me involved with the Olympics and for being a true well-rounded friend (not just kicking my butt in Ironman races). You are an inspiration.

J. P. ROSATO: You give me energy and strength every time we talk. Thank you for being a pillar of strength in the trenches with me for over 15 years.

CHARLES SAMUEL: You are the pillar of strength all across Asia. I'm grateful for your heart of gold and pearls of wisdom.

SARAH: Thanks for always understanding conceptually what is needed when, where, and why.

SHELLY: Thank you for keeping it all together and helping me daily. You are an angel from heaven—no more words needed!

BRANDON SHIN: Thank you for always putting me back together, for over a dozen years now. You're more than just a hairstylist; you help ground me whenever I see you.

ERIN STORIE: You're a wonderful example of grinding it out daily as an Olympian and training hard for your results. I love your dedication and focus.

ROBB SUCHER: Thank you for putting your life on the line daily and showing what real grit and grind is all about in the military. I will never forget meeting you at Fleet Week at Winged Foot.

JOE THEISMANN: Thanks for being the ultimate football hero when I was growing up. I remember watching you get injured then get back up and give it your all on the field each week. I'm grateful to have had those conversations with you at the Super Bowl. I hope to see you there for many years to come.

LAURIE TOSCANO: Thanks for being with me on all the business trips around the world. There's no one I'd rather eat breadsticks with from meeting to meeting. I've watched you blossom into who you are and am so proud of you.

PETE TRIZZINO: We've grown up in the industry together and worked side-by-side during multiple incidents. I appreciate your friendship and your business acumen of diving into the daily details. I am so proud of you.

CRAIG VITALE AND LIZ TREMAIN: Thanks for being my amazing triathlon coaches. Your lives are full of discipline, and you push yourselves to the limit training and racing. Thank you for all of the encouragement and support. Even when we all fall in an Ironman race, we get back up. You're both so inspiring.

RAY WANG: Thank you for always innovating and being true to who you are. And thanks for taking the motto "No assholes" into the C-Suite.

ROSHUMBA WILLIAMS: Thanks for your sisterhood and positive light, and for being a pillar of strength throughout life events and moments. I'm grateful that we have so much in common and we're able to grind out life together. I admire all you have done.

WINGED FOOT GOLF CLUB FRIENDS: You know who you are. Thank you for always bringing a smile to my face and for being a safe haven. I treasure our many laughs in the NIBBS grillroom.

TO ALL MY CLOSEST GIRLFRIENDS (YOU KNOW WHO YOU ARE): Thank you for always ensuring we get together to make memories every year. The Girlfriend Gown Gala was a night I'll never forget. And thanks for laughing at me (and playing along) each year when events have to be planned out a year in advance.

TO ALL THE PEOPLE I'VE MENTORED: You are some of the reasons I work so hard. It's important to me that each of you knows who you are and how important you are in my life. Never stop learning and living!

Finally, THANK YOU to everyone on teams I have led or managed around the world. Each of you has made an impact on me. Remember, I will always work for you, and I am proud to be your leader.

ABOUT THE AUTHOR

RHONDA VETERE is a global, seasoned C-Suite technology executive who has worked across industries in the technology field. A change agent for digital transformation, she has led the way for growth with more than 23 mergers and acquisitions at various companies.

A passionate leader in technology across industries, Rhonda has worked in global executive positions at Estée Lauder Companies, AIG, HP Enterprise Services, Barclays/Lehman Brothers, Bank One/JPMorgan Chase, CompuServe, UUNET, MCI, and Worldcom. She has lived and worked internationally—in New York, Hong Kong, Singapore, London, Mumbai, and across India—and has managed teams of more than 20,000 people.

As an industry expert and influencer, Vetere has been a keynote speaker and panelist at many conferences and events, including the World Economic Forum/Davos, WIT (Women in Technology) Connect, Microsoft Global CIO Summit, Dell EMC World, and the US Vice Presidential Candidate Debate. She has been recognized for her leadership and influence, notably with a 2017 Stevie Award for Excellence in Transforming Business and as a multiyear Top 100 CIO/CTO Executive Leader in STEM by STEMconnector.

An avid sports fan and real-world corporate athlete, Rhonda stays focused and sharp by competing in marathons and triathlons on a regular basis—over 70 events thus far, including 70.3-mile Ironman triathlons. She recently made history by running 55 miles in the Serengeti as part of a girls' and women's empowerment fundraiser, the first women-only run of its kind.

We hope you enjoyed *Grit & Grind*.

DISCOUNTS AVAILABLE FOR BULK ORDERS!

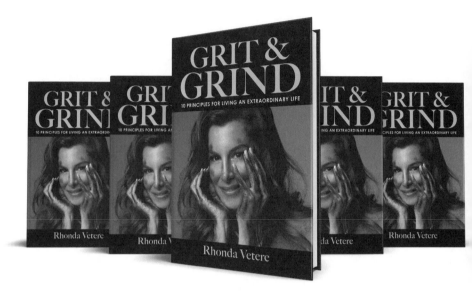

Share *Grit & Grind* with your...

- School

- Organization

- Employees

For ordering information, contact: Sales@thanethousebooks.com.

Want to bring this message to your organization?

Rhonda Vetere is available for speaking engagements.

For booking details, contact the publisher:
Sales@ThanetHousebooks.com.

THANET HOUSE PUBLISHING helps mission-driven business people write and publish books that change the world. By creating master messaging and keystone frameworks, we're able to create a wide range of written materials that Inspire, Educate, and Sell.

Check us out at www.thanethousebooks.com.